The
Politically
IN Correct
Cookbook

The Facts, Fantasies and Fallacies
of the
Endangered Species Act

by Karl W. Drexel
Illustrations by Fitzhugh

Whitney-Hill • Santa Rosa • California

Edited by Roxanne Wright
Cover Design and Computer Art by Jerry Moffitt, Cotati, CA
Back Cover Photography by Roxanne Wright
Clipart Copyright ©1995 by Zedcor, Inc., Reprinted with permission
Calvin and Hobbes Copyright ©1995 by Universal Press Syndicate,
        Reprinted with permission

Printed and bound by Barlow Printing, Cotati, CA

ISBN: 0-9650435-0-9

Published in the United States by
Whitney-Hill
P.O. Box 2910
Santa Rosa, CA 95405

This is dedicated to Roxanne, to whom I am eternally grateful for her untiring support, encouragement and occasional prodding, without which I could not have completed this book.

Thank you to the one I love.

ACKNOWLEDGMENTS

It takes a tremendous amount of help to put together a book like this, and I cannot begin to list all of the people responsible for its completion. However, I would like to thank those many sources who provided me with information, documentation, and assistance, without whom my research would have taken many more than the five years spent.

My thanks to Adrienne Roberts, American Forest and Paper Association; Kathleen S. Creason, M.B.A., California Mining Association; Sharon A. Simmons, Temperate Forest Foundation; Elizabeth M. Pease, National Hardwood Lumber Association; Dennis Hollingsworth, Riverside County Farm Bureau; R.J. Smith, Competitive Enterprise Institute; Richard Stroup, Political Economy Research Center; William Perry Pendley, Mountain States Legal Foundation; Mary Murphy, Western Building Materials Association; David Cutler, Merchant Magazine and Building Products Digest; Debra Baker, Southern Timber Purchasers Association; Ted James, AICP, Kern County, CA, Resource Management Agency; Ike Sugg, Competitive Enterprise Institute; Richard L. Krause, American Farm Bureau Federation; Daniel T. Fitzpatrick, Pacific Legal Foundation; Robert D. Thornton, Nossaman, Gunther, Knox & Elliott.

I also want to thank Lily, Chris, and Nick of Old Vic's in Santa Rosa, for allowing us to use "our" table, where this book was inspired, edited, updated, proofed, and discussed as the book took shape.

Thank you to Jessie, Janice, Jane, Ann, Debbie and Kathy for their assistance. To Roxanne for the photography and the many hours of editing. To Jerry Moffitt for his computer talents and help. To Michael and Merna of the New Lena's in Santa Rosa, for their support.

I also want to extend a special thanks to Universal Press Syndicate for permission to re-print "Calvin and Hobbes".

And a special hearty thank you to Pat Barlow of Barlow Printing for all his help in getting this book to you.

KWD

CONTENTS

Preface   ix

In The Beginning   1

The Endangered Species Act of 1973   5

    The Noah Principle   10

    Costs   15

    Private Property Rights   23

    Agenda   25

    Solutions   32

Recipes   45

Conclusion   145

Sources   151

Index   161

PREFACE

· This is not really a cookbook in the popular sense of the word, rather it is an attempt to educate the public of the true facts, fantasies, and fallacies of the Endangered Species Act. Facts that are not commonly known by the general public, but in reality affect each and every one of us. It is my belief, that through knowledge, we might be able to make reasonable decisions on legislation that can combine economic, personal, and cultural factors with our commitment for proper stewardship of this planet.

I have researched and collected information for the last five years to compile this collection of data. None of it is my own, rather it is a compilation of scientific facts, real stories, and economic statistics presented by professionals from many, many sources.

I was inspired to compile this information by the excessive misuse and abuse that has been accomplished by preservationist groups to further their personal agendas. This abuse of what has been termed a "good law that has gone haywire" has in fact encouraged private land owners to abandon their good stewardship of the land in order to protect their private property for future generations. It has become a constant battlefield for litigation that is, in reality, a lose-lose situation. Nobody wins in

the long run, especially the fragile species the law was intended
to protect. And guess what? You and I ultimately foot the bill.

I was also inspired by an article written by a fourteen year
old girl, printed in a local newspaper, regarding her belief of the
imminent demise of all plant and animal life on this planet. Her
beliefs were truly from the heart and I admire her for that,
however, her article was filled with misinformation, propaganda
and unwarranted hysteria. The most alarming statement coming
from the article was, and I quote, "I wish that Homo erectus and
Homo sapien never evolved on this planet." Is this what the
doomsday hysteria has come to? Where is the balance, the logic
or the intelligence we want our young people to grow and mature
with? Where is the common sense?

I hope that I can bring at least a little common sense to
some of the people through this light-hearted, and, indeed at
times, satirical look at what was once a good idea -- The
Endangered Species Act.

kwd
1995

IN THE BEGINNING

In the Age of Dinosaurs, which began 205 million years ago (MYA), the dinosaurs and other ancient reptiles roamed the Earth. These amazing creatures continued to rule the planet for 140 million years, until they mysteriously died out 65 MYA. During this time the world saw many changes: continents moved, sea levels altered, climates changed (real global warming and global cooling at maximum levels), and many new creatures and plants appeared while others became extinct.

There were probably over 400 different types of dinosaurs, and the greatest number of different dinosaur types has been found in North America, Europe, and Asia.

Over the last 65 million years, marine and land animals have been disappearing and appearing. Dinosaurs, and their cousins Pterosaurs (the "winged lizard") disappeared, along with the swimming reptiles, Plesiosaurs. So, too, did the Delemnites and Ammonites -- two ancient groups of relatives of octopus and squid. The extinction made way for development and evolution of a modern mixture of animal types. We can see them all around us today -- mammals, birds, lizards, crocodiles, turtles, fish, snails, and shellfish.

As long as there are living plants, animals, and microbes on Earth, the slow but steady process of evolution will continue. While the process of evolution makes new types of living things --

able to adapt to their changing environment -- other sorts are disappearing as they become extinct. It's been going on for millions of years, and will continue, regardless of man's futile and unrealistic attempt to save every living thing from extinction. Dr. Phillip Whitfield in his book, *Why did the Dinosaurs Disappear?*, says, "In the addition sum of nature, the total number of species of living things usually stays about the same."

As noted scientist Bjorn Kurten, in his anthology on cave bears explains, most of the species that ever existed on Earth are now extinct. Some died out because their "niche" vanished -- that combination of environmental factors and adaptive response that kept the species going. Two good examples today are the Federally protected Iowa Pleistocene snail and the Wyoming toad, generally considered relicts of the glacial era, that will never be restored or thrive unless their is another Ice Age! Other species have disappeared because their niche was conquered by a superior competitor. Still others became extinct because of degeneration, a less specialized or less functional form through retrospective evolution.

The evolution and extinction of species has been going on since time began. Animals move from place to place and adapt to new environments. As one species moves out, another species is able to move in. This evolution and adaptation is part of a larger plan orchestrated and designed for a greater purpose.

Over the last 65 million years, there were four major Ice Ages making land travel possible. As the dinosaurs vanished, lesser animals were able to move into new territory and adapt to their new environments. During the second of these Ice Ages, black bear, mule deer, beaver, bison, and mammoths came from Asia to North America over what is now the Bering Strait. Musk oxen, wolly mammoths, reindeer, ermine, timber wolves, moose, elk, otter, and red fox traveled the same direction during the third Ice Age about 250,000 years ago.

During the fourth Ice Age, some 80,000 years ago, more animals traversed the land bridge from Asia to North America -- the arctic fox, grizzly bear and polar bear, snowshoe hare, mountain goat and big horn sheep. The Yak and Saiga antelope came too, but they later became extinct in North America.

An excellent example of movement, adaptation, evolution, and extinction was noted in a recent addition of National Geographic. It seems the wolly mammoth moved into North America, and some found their way to what is now Southern California. The large mammoths stood about 14 feet tall at the shoulder, and lived on the mainland of the continent. It is presumed by scientists, that at some point during one of the Ice Ages, these full sized mammoths swam to the Channel Islands when the sea level was lower and the Islands formed a single land mass. As the ice melted and the sea level rose, dividing the islands, the mammoths were left with fewer resources, giving smaller animals an evolutionary edge. The fossil remains of what is called a Dwarf mammoth were recently discovered on Santa Rosa Island, California, part of the Channel Island chain. This smaller mammoth, that stood only 5-6 feet high at the shoulder, had evolved into a smaller animal more able to adapt to the new environment. At some point in time, tens of thousands of years ago, it too became extinct.

This example of evolution and adaptation was reported in the National Geographic, as I mentioned. What is even more remarkable, however, is a report in the same issue describing the discovery of a *new* species. John MacKinnon, a World Wildlife Fund biologist, and a group of Vietnamese researchers, found three partial skulls of the Sao La during a survey of the Vu Quang Nature Reserve in central Vietnam, in 1992. DNA analysis confirmed that it was a previously unknown species. A couple of years later, farmers found a live Sao La female (similar to a small deer), and it was taken to a botanical garden in Hanoi for study. It died within about four months of respiratory and digestive problems, but it gave scientist a look at what may be a new emerging species that is evolving and trying to adapt to a new environment.

The most highly developed traveler of all during the last Ice Age, the culmination of evolution and adaptation, was Man.

This mammal, walking upright, on two feet, with a large evolved cranial capacity, opposing thumbs, and big toes is *Homo sapien sapien*, anatomically modern humans; us; human beings. Destined, designed and evolved to be a technologically innovative people. Destined to build shelter, grow and raise food, discover ore and experience a place called home. After all, sapien is derived from the Latin word meaning wise or knowledge.

THE ENDANGERED SPECIES ACT OF 1973

What is the Endangered Species Act of 1973 (ESA)? Where did it come from, and why does it exist? Why do some feel it is the greatest accomplishment of the conservation movement, and others believe it is a "law gone haywire"? Why do some people swear by it, and others swear at it? In order to understand the facts, fantasies, and fallacies of the ESA, we need to look back at the political climate and the origins of this Act.

After establishing the first National Park in 1872 -- Yellowstone National Park -- and Yosemite National Park in 1890, Congress decided in all their wisdom to form a bureaucracy to oversee these Parks and to establish a nationwide network of National Parks. Thus in 1906, the first Act of Title 16 of the United States Codes was enacted. This Act was called "National Parks, Military Parks, Monuments, and Seashores", and is designated as Chapter One of Title 16. (Title 16 of the USC is called simply -- Conservation, and all the US laws enacted since that time dealing with conservation fall under Title 16.) Since 1906, and the National Park Service Act of 1916, the parks system has grown to include 368 parks, monuments, and historical sights covering over 80 million acres. This is just under Chapter 1 of Title 16.

Subsequent to the establishment of the National Park system, an additional ninety-six (96) separate conservation Acts have been enacted by Congress, encompassed in sixty-three (63) separate Chapters of Title 16. Some of the more widely known Acts that have been enacted are National Forests Act (Chapter 2), Protection of Fur Seals and Other Fur-Bearing Animals Act (Chapter 5), Protection and Conservation of Wildlife (Chapter 5A), Game and Bird Preserves; Protection (Chapter 6), Protection of Migratory Game and Insectivorous Birds (Chapter 7), and Chapter 9 established the Fish and Wildlife Service to interpret and enforce these laws of the land. Some of these laws became quite specific in their intent, such as the Northern Pacific Halibut Fishing Act (Chapter 10), Regulation of Whaling Act (Chapter 14), Whale Conservation and Protection (Chapter 14A), Atlantic Tuna Fishing (Chapter 16A), Eastern Pacific Tuna Fishing (Chapter 16B), South Pacific Tuna Fishing (Chapter 16C), and my all-time favorite, "Jellyfish or Sea Nettles, Other Such Pests, and Seaweed in Coastal Waters: Control or Elimination Act" (Chapter 25).

Many of these seemingly important and productive laws also seem to overlap in their emphasis and purpose. We have, for example, Protection of Fur Seals and Other Fur-Bearing Animals (Chapter 5), as well as Conservation and Protection of North Pacific Fur Seals (Chapter 24); Whale Conservation and Protection Act (Chapter 14A), along with the Marine Mammal Protection Act of 1972 (Chapter 31), and Marine Sanctuaries (Chapter 32); Wild Horses and Burros: Protection, Management, and Control Act (Chapter 30), when we already have Protection and Conservation of Wildlife (Chapter 5A). Another apparent duplication is the Fishery Conservation and Management Act (Chapter 38), Fish and Wildlife Conservation (Chapter 49), Salmon and Steelhead Conservation and Enhancement (Chapter 52), Pacific Salmon Fishing Act (Chapter 56A), and the National Fish and Wildlife Foundation (Chapter 57). And after all of that we have been blessed with the Fish and Seafood Promotion Act (Chapter 60).

Following the environmental movement of the 1960's, Congress enacted numerous conservation Acts, some of which I have already discussed, but the grand-daddy of all, the culmination of environmental hysteria, the all encompassing catch-all of conservation, was Chapter 35, the Endangered Species Act of 1973. It was passed by a sweeping majority in both Houses of Congress, by both political parties. Seldom before had a bill received such bipartisan support and had such overwhelming support from the public in general. The bill was signed, readily and with great fanfare, by the President of the United States, Richard M. Nixon. However, in just over 20 years, this bill has become the most divisive law this country has seen since Prohibition.

One of the authors of the Act, Senator Mark Hatfield of Oregon, was quoted in *The Washington Post* on June 12, 1992, as saying, "I have supported -- and continue to support -- the Endangered Species Act. I helped write it. I offered the 1972 version of the act that eventually became law in 1973. I want it to survive." Senator Hatfield continued with "...today the act is being applied across entire states and regions, with the result that it now affects millions upon millions of acres of publicly and privately owned land, and many thousands of human beings...The fact is that Congress always considered the human element as central to the success of the ESA...The situation has gotten out of control."

The passage of the Endangered Species Act, was a well intentioned move to provide a program for the conservation of endangered and threatened species. The US Fish and Wildlife Service (FWS) was empowered to collect scientific data as it related to threatened or endangered species, list the species as threatened or endangered, implement a program for their recovery, and de-list those species that become recovered. All this is well and good, providing FWS follows these very important guidelines. As we will see however, this is not always the case.

In "theory", an animal or plant determined to be in danger is placed on the Endangered Species list by the US Fish and Wildlife Service. It is then monitored, protected and recovered, before finally being removed from the list. In practice, however, no case exists in which it can be legitimately stated that a species' condition improved to the point that it was removed from the list as a result of the act's implementation. According to the National Wilderness Institute, as of 1992, less than 10% of all listed species had reached more than half of their "recovery criteria". Only five species have been officially claimed as "recovered", but in all cases "data error" -- listing of the species in the first place was a mistake -- or factors unrelated to this law were the actual reason for their "recovery".

Conservationists' groups like to tout the recovery of the Bald Eagle as an example of the success of the ESA. First it perpetuates the myth that the Act works, and secondly and probably most importantly it provides fodder for pleas of donations. In an article from *The New York Times*, the Bald Eagle was described as one of "the law's notable successes". The article in the June 30, 1994 edition, entitled "*Eagles Fly Free of the Endangered List*", credits the listing of the eagle on the Endangered Species List for its resurgence. Joan Guifoyle, of the US Fish and Wildlife Service was quoted as saying "The Endangered Species Act was the tool that enabled us to make the eagle's recovery an active process." The truth of the matter is, the eagle was already on the way to recovery before it was listed, and the primary reason for its recovery was the banning of DDT in 1972. The population of adult pairs of Bald Eagles in 1963 was listed as 417. In 1974 -- two years after the ban on DDT, but a full four years before the eagle was listed on the endangered species list -- that population had almost doubled to 791 pairs. The Bald Eagle was listed in 1978, and three short years later -- before the ESA could have had an effect, and before even a recovery plan had been designed -- the population had jumped to 1,188, almost triple the population in less than twenty years. It's no wonder from that population base, the Bald Eagle in the lower 48 states has swelled to over 4,000 nesting pairs, with an estimated 45,000 more eagles in Alaska, but it is naive (or "politically correct") to give credit to the Endangered Species Act.

This same article continued to espouse the merits of the ESA, and continuing the mythical successes, by saying the Gray Whale was another of the many recoveries attributed to the ESA, when in fact it's recovery is due entirely to the Marine Mammal Act that preceded the ESA, and the Gray Whale was in fact recovering prior to the enactment of the Marine Mammal Act. The whooping crane population has increased to 17 times its level of the 1940's, but it was protected twenty years before the Endangered Species Act was introduced. The Peregrine Falcon is another species that has recovered primarily due to the ban of DDT in 1972, and yet proponents of the ESA continue to point to these species as real success stories of the Act.

Until recently, many people thought the Endangered Species Act was passed to protect majestic creatures such as Bald Eagles, Grizzly Bears, and Gray Whales. And, clearly, most people are willing to bear some costs in the attempt to conserve such species. I certainly don't think anybody is against the preservation of species, or the sanctity of life. It is the inadequacies of the Endangered Species Act itself, and the inflexibility of its interpretation, as well as the abusive misuse of its intent, that needs to be addressed. We aren't talking about "charismatic megafauna" anymore. Now, the Fish and Wildlife Service, responsible for the implementation of the Endangered Species Act, has listed 955 species of plants and animals and has 4,000 more under consideration. Of those animals classified as candidates for future listing, 70% of them are snails, spiders, insects, mussels, and other invertebrates.

In addition, as part of a settlement of a lawsuit brought by several conservation groups, the FWS has agreed to list approximately 400 more species by 1996, listing 120 in 1994 alone, and will, according to the Wilderness Society "expedite the listing of some 900 more species believed [by these groups] to warrant listing but for which no definitive scientific evidence has been produced." We need to get a handle on reality if we are going to be able to conserve and preserve anything. Mr. Robert Legg, of the Temperate Forest Foundation, made the point very succinct when he wrote, "the truth is, we don't have an unlimited amount of money to spend, and by spending a little bit on everything, we accomplish almost nothing."

The Noah Principle

A biologist, David Ehrenfeld, has advanced a theory called the "Noah Principle", which says we have to take everything on the ark with us as we go forward. This theory says that the smallest grub and the largest whale have equal rights and protection, and must be saved at any cost. Are we, as the stewards of this planet, supposed to stop the evolutionary process, and preserve everything that exists? Even God only commanded Noah to collect species "two by two."

The definition, listed in Title 16 Chapter 35, "The Endangered Species Act", for the term "fish or wildlife" is as follows:

> *Any member of the animal kingdom including without limitation any mammal, fish, bird (including any migratory, nonmigratory, or endangered bird for which protection is also afforded by treaty or other international agreement), amphibian, reptile, mollusk, crustacean, anthropod or other invertebrate, and includes any part, product, egg, or offspring thereof, or the dead body parts thereof.*

The definition of plants in the wording of the ESA is:

Any member of the plant kingdom, including seeds, roots, and other parts thereof.

Harvard professor and renowned entomologist, E.O. Wilson, estimates that there may be as many as 100,000,000 species of plants and animals in the world, of which only about 1,400,000 have been identifled. Homo sapien is one species, of about 4,000, of the class Mammals -- a category of life on the decline over the last 200 million years. As members of the order Primate, we belong to a grouping that today numbers about 200 species (a number that has declined from its peak several million years ago). In comparison, the number of insect species is 15,000,000. As Wilson so aptly put it, " God seems to have had a fondness for beetles". The Endangered Species Act does not discriminate or differentiate, and all species gets equal protection under the law.

If vertebrates are just the tip of the iceberg in species diversity, and invertebrates are just as important, then we have a mighty big iceberg coming at us. In fact, in the forests of the Pacific Northwest alone -- an area targeted by preservationists with the spotted owl and marbled murrelet -- scientists have found 527 species of fungi, 157 lichens, 106 mosses, 130 vascular plants, 350 mollusks, 750 anthropods, 314 salmonids, 62 amphibians, 38 birds, 15 mammals, and 15 species of bats.

If we apply the "Noah Principle" to these figures, and try to save every species of plant and animal that exists, the economic, social, and cultural cost to human beings would be catastrophic. It seems that Groucho Marx could have been talking about the Endangered Species Act when he said, "Politics is the art of looking for trouble, finding it everywhere, diagnosing it incorrectly, and applying the wrong remedies".

The Endangered Species Act doesn't stop with just species to be protected, either. According to the definition listed in the body of the Act, "the term 'species' includes any sub-species of fish or wildlife or plants, and any *distinct population segment* of any species of vertebrate, fish or wildlife which interbreeds when mature". (Emphasis added) Science, on the other hand, acknowledges individual variations within a species and defines species simply as a group of interbreeding or potentially interbreeding organisms that are reproductively isolated from other such groups, and can produce fertile offspring. (ie: lions reproduce only with lions, chimpanzees only with chimpanzees).

By adding the "distinct population segment" to the equation, the Act removes itself from real scientific classification and opens its interpretation to sentiment and emotion, allowing several groups of the same species to be considered independently of the others in order to achieve the listing as threatened or endangered, when in fact that is not the case.

An example of how this classification system works is exemplified in the Central Valley of California with the kangaroo rat. If we acknowledge that the kangaroo rat is a distinct species, or even a sub-species, then we know that they can interbreed and produce fertile offspring. However, there are five different "distinct populations" listed on the threatened or endangered species lists, based on their geographical location. There is the Fresno Kangaroo Rat, Giant Kangaroo Rat, Stephen's Kangaroo Rat, Tipton Kangaroo Rat, and most recently, Merriam's Kangaroo Rat. There is even a Hermann Kangaroo Rat that has not been listed as endangered, probably because humans don't farm, log, mine or build houses where the Hermann dwells.

Another example of this highly subjective way of classifying species, is the Santa Cruz Fox. Found on an island off the coast of California, this "subspecies" is one of five other subspecies listed, one each for the five other islands nearby. Yet experts consider that all these constitute a single species of gray fox whose range is from the East to the West Coast and into

Mexico -- a species that is abundant and certainly not facing extinction.

This way of distinguishing species could be likened to our saying that a brown-haired, blue-eyed, white male living in Redding, California is a distinctly different population than a brown-haired, brown-eyed, white female living in Phoenix, Arizona. When in fact, they could, if they desired, interbreed and produce fertile offspring, and thus, by scientific definition, be defined as the same species (which we all know to be the case). However, if you take all of the different segments of a species separately, and classify them as distinct populations, the percentage of those segments to the total population will obviously be reduced, and an argument can be made that because the percentage to the total population is so low, the species must be threatened..

In their book, *Noah's Choice: The Future of Endangered Species*, Charles C. Mann and Mark L. Plummer, both scientists and contributors to *Science* and *The Atlantic Monthly*, argue that trying to save every species is unethical and impractical, that we have to make choices. When the Endangered Species Act was passed in 1973, few people -- least of all, Congress -- understood its ramifications, especially the cost.

The Act charges the Fish and Wildlife Service with protecting every endangered species in the US, no matter what the cost. The battle over the number of jobs threatened, or private property idled by endangered species is irrelevant, because the law doesn't care. One job or 100,000 jobs, one acre or 1,000 acres -- it doesn't matter. Any one owl, rat, salamander, or beetle still comes ahead of all human interests, and there is no affective way to balance matters. Once a species is listed on the endangered or threatened species list, then each single plant or animal (or part thereof), alive or dead, is protected with the same inflexible mania.

The Government cannot legally single out some species as economically valuable, or ecologically important, and devote more resources to saving them. Nor can it let others vanish. It is committed to the fiction that we can save each and every one. While trying to take all the species with us on the ark, many more species will disappear, as well as many more jobs, personal property rights, and even human rights, along with them. There is no reason to believe that the hard choices that need to be made, of which species and which jobs to let go, will be made in a meaningful way. Thus, the battles will continue, every side losing, until the Endangered Species Act is changed.

The late Dixie Lee Ray was the "intellectual foundation" for the movement to inject reason and solid science back into the field of environmental policy. In her book, *Environmental Overkill: Whatever Happened to Common Sense*, she so aptly put the current problem into perspective, when she said, "The preservation and protection of all wetlands (and all species, and sub-species that exist today) is a fine example of good intentions gone wild; of our propensity to cure everything with legislation, and of our inability to see the ultimate consequences of ill-considered actions based more on sentiment and emotion than on sound science and logic. What ever happened to common sense?"

And what about sound science? As the law is written, anybody with an agenda, with a biologist on staff, can petition the Fish and Wildlife Service to have a species listed as threatened or endangered. The FWS must then hold hearings and use the "scientific" data presented to make a decision. It is mandated to make that decision with the "best scientific information available" at the time. Often times this is inadequate, outdated and even biased information, and it is up to the scientific community at large to "disprove" this slanted "scientific data", or the FWS will rule in favor of the listing. This is exactly what happened with the Spotted Owl in 1990. Even though there is overwhelming scientific data that has been presented by new and continuing studies, proving that the species is not threatened or endangered, the US Fish and Wildlife Service refuses to de-list it, rather opting to let the courts and Congress decide its fate.

And what of logic? Where are we, as taxpayers, going to get the hundreds of millions of dollars being spent, and the billions of dollars forecasted as needed, on implementing the Endangered Species Act as it now exists? And as more and more jobs are lost, and companies close, and entire industries are strangled, from where are the tax dollars going to come?

Costs

If in fact the Endangered Species Act of 1973, with all of its subsequent amendments, actually worked in reality, it would still behoove us all, and our Representatives in Congress, to look at and analyze the costs. The direct and indirect costs, in purely monetary figures alone, is staggering.

The Federal Government spends a total of $21.8 billion in what is classified in the Federal Budget as National Resources/Environment. In the 1995 budget of the Federal Government, that represents slightly less than Public Health ($27.0 billion), Food Stamps ($26.2 billion), and Welfare (AFDC, SSI, etc. at $25.1 billion). It is more than the Federal Government spends on International Affairs ($21.0 billion), Administration of Justice ($17.3 billion), Science ($16.9 billion), General Government ($13.8 billion), Community and Regional Development ($9.2 billion), and Energy Research and Development ($4.6 billion). In fact, in the 1995 Federal Budget, National Resources-/Environment was budgeted more than the last ten budget items combined, including Child Nutrition, Agriculture, WIC, Student Loans, and all of the National Endowment Programs.

Certainly not all of the $21.8 billion is allocated to support and enforce the Endangered Species Act. In fact, direct federal expenses to uphold the premise of the Act, falls far short of what is necessary for it to function in its present structure properly.

The Fish and Wildlife Service, which is the primary source for the enforcement of the Endangered Species Act, budgeted almost $89 million for recovery, consultation, law enforcement, listing and permits related to the ESA in the 1995 budget. This was a 32% increase over the 1994 budget, and does not include the additional $10.6 million for the Cooperative Endangered Species Fund or the $978,000 for Endangered Species Fisheries. This budget, in fact, contributes to a total of almost $300 million in appropriated Federal funds over the last four years that doesn't even have Congressional authorization, since the ESA has not been re-authorized by Congress since 1992. According to the rules of the House of Representatives, Federal programs not officially authorized, or reauthorized by law, should not receive funding. However, this rule has been conveniently ignored by Congress since 1992.

So where does the money go? How is it dispersed among the almost 950 listed species, and how successfully has the money, that has been spent, worked for recovery?

Determining the actual total cost of the Endangered Species Act is almost impossible, and is certainly beyond the scope of this book. In fact, the Government does not even have an estimate of the total cost of the Act. The US Fish and Wildlife Service, primarily, and the National Marine Fisheries Service, secondarily, are responsible for implementing the Endangered Species Act. However, other Federal, State, and Local agencies also spend large sums of money on endangered species. In 1992, State and Federal agencies, other than FWS and NMFS, made nearly 94% of the expenditures on the ten species receiving the most funding that year.

Not all expenditures are identified as direct costs to the Endangered Species Act, but none the less are directly a result of its implementation. Hundreds of millions of dollars spent on studies, legal fees, mitigation fees, litigation costs, interest on loans caused by delays and lost revenues, are not included in most identified and reported costs related to the ESA.

The Endangered Species Act was designed to conserve plants or animals endangered with extinction. Under the Act, conserve means recovering a plant or animal to the point where it can be taken off the list. The first step in the recovery process is a detailed recovery plan produced by the Fish and Wildlife

Serviced or the National Marine Fisheries Service, listing the steps necessary to improve the status of a listed plant or animal. A comprehensive study of 306 recovery plans, released by the National Wilderness Institute in 1993, revealed some staggering figures. The plans that were studied included 8 amphibians, 72 birds, 57 fish, 58 invertebrates, 35 mammals, 135 plants and 23 reptiles, covering 388 of the endangered and threatened species listed at that time. Based on the plans reviewed, the total identifiable costs of these plans, from the original listing to the study, was $884,164,000. This figure only represents the cost for these 306 plans under study and does not represent the costs for: actions called for in recovery plans for which costs are not estimated; costs of recovery for the additional 500+ species already listed, but not covered by one of the plans reviewed; costs of recovery for the 4,000 official candidates and proposed species which will be added to the endangered species list; costs of reduced or terminated business activities and jobs lost as a result of conflict; or lost federal, state, and local tax revenue.

In addition, many recovery plan cost estimates do not accurately reflect actual government expenditures. One example is the Schaus swallowtail butterfly. Total identifiable costs estimated in the recovery plan submitted by the Fish and Wildlife Service to bring this butterfly to full recovery (and thus de-listing), was $128,000. However, between 1989 and 1991 alone, federal and state expenditures on this species exceeded that amount by 1,107 percent. Similarly, federal and state expenditures on the Florida scrub jay exceeded its total determined recovery plan costs in the same three year period by 33,340 percent.

The study by the National Wilderness Institute lists the costs for the ten most expensive recovery plans, from the initial listing through 1993, as follows:

Atlantic Green Turtle	$88,236,000
Loggerhead Turtle	85,947,000
Blunt-Nosed Leopard Lizard	70,252,000

Colorado Squaw Fish	57,770,000
Humpback Chub	
Bonytail Chub	
Razorback Sucker	
Black-Capped Vireo	53,538,000
Swamp Pink	29,026,000

The most expensive recovery plan in the study was the $88,236,000 spent on the Atlantic Green Turtle, and the average cost of all the plans studied was $3,059,391. Total identifiable costs of just the 306 plans studied was $884,164,000. If we use just the average cost figure, times the 4,500 species not included in those costs, we are looking at government expenditures of $13,767,259,500!

In a paper written in 1994 by Andrew Metrick and Martin Weitzman of Harvard University, the spending patterns and the distribution of funds by the Fish and Wildlife Service, shows that not all species get equal or even rational treatment. The portent of the Endangered Species Act is that unlimited costs should be borne to protect each endangered creature equally. However, in reality, there is a perverse priority system that is in place to distribute the budgeted allocations. This study, like the National Wilderness Institute study, only reflects the identifiable federal (and some state) expenditures on a species by species basis. It does not include amounts that cannot be assigned to individual species, and does not include the far greater costs imposed on the private sector or other government agencies.

The top 10 species receiving the most money for recovery, during a three year period from 1989-1991, are mostly mammals and birds. They received 54% of the $316,850,000 spent on all endangered or threatened species listed during this period. They include

Bald Eagle	$31,300,000
Northern Spotted Owl	26,400,000
Florida Scrubjay	19,900,000

West Indian Manatee	17,300,000
Red-Cockaded Woodpecker	15,100,000
Florida Panther	13,600,000
Grizzly (or Brown) Bear	12,600,000
Least Bell's Vireo	12,500,000
American Peregrine Falcon	11,600,000
Whooping Crane	10,800,000

This study also asserts that there is some doubt that these species are truly endangered, or even threatened, in any objective scientific sense. The Bald Eagle, Northern Spotted Owl, Florida Scrubjay, and Grizzly Bear, for example, have relatively large viable breeding populations, that, while being pressed upon in some places, do not appear to be remotely exposed to any overall danger of going extinct. However, the same cannot be said of the Texas Blind Salamander, Monito Gecko, Choctawahatchee Beach Mouse, or Waccamaw Silverside, which are much closer to extinction, but for any one, less than $10,000 was spent during this 3 year period.

Furthermore, only four of the top 10 are species (Bald Eagle, West Indian Manatee, Whooping Crane, and Red-Cockaded Woodpecker). The other six are sub-species, which have closely related, almost genetically identical, twin sub-species that are in no danger at all of going extinct. At the other extreme, however, there are the Sand Skink, Red Hills Salamander, and Alabama Cavefish. Less than $10,000 was spent on each of these species, yet each species forms a monotypic genus - meaning they are the genetically distinct unique representative of an entire genus, having no twin sister species, or even closely related cousin species.

The basic finding in the Metrick and Weitzman study, according to Harvard economics professor and Fellow at the Hoover Institute, Robert J. Barro, is that not all species are getting equal treatment. In fact, after listing a species as endangered or threatened, the level of threat and the degree of uniqueness (measured by whether the protected animal is a unique monotypic genus, a species, or a subspecies), has absolutely no role in determining how much money is allocated and to which animal.

Whatever the merits of preserving animals, the Endangered Species Act has to be viewed as a curious piece of legislation. On the one hand, the Act pretends that unlimited costs should be borne to protect each endangered or threatened creature, including the taking of private property without compensation. On the other hand, in actual practice, the priority system applied by government spending suggests that popularity counts more than endangerment or uniqueness.

In addition to USFWS and NMFS, additional federal, state, and local agencies spend millions of dollars annually in support of endangered species. A partial list compiled by the National Wilderness Institute, from documents reported to FWS, shows spending by agencies reporting over $100,000 in annual expenditures and the number of species affected:

FEDERAL

Animal and Plant Health Inspection Services	$ 1,049,233	36 Species
Army Corps of Engineers	83,368,400	161 Species
Bureau of Indian Affairs	2,960,700	31 Species
Bureau of Land Management	2,390,600	68 Species
Bureau of Reclamation	23,248,000	54 Species
Dept. of Air Force	3,427,300	33 Species
Dept. of Army	4,788,300	27 Species
Dept. of Navy	2,754,500	46 Species
EPA	3,068,244	130 Species
Federal Highway Admin.	13,700,000	16 Species
Forest Service	25,833,300	190 Species
Nat'l Marine Fisheries Service	5,876,200	15 Species
Nat'l Park Service	3,830,200	77 Species

STATE

Cumulative Total for
Expenditures Over
$100,000 per Species $127,697,600   26 Species

As the FWS stated in their 1992 report (latest available), the information presented:

> *"Does not reflect the total national effort...and continues to present an incomplete funding picture. A significant portion of threatened and endangered species conservation activities includes law enforcement, consultation, recovery coordination, and other actions that are not easily or reasonably identified to species. Accounting procedures by all agencies for most staff salaries, operations, maintenance, and other support services are not recorded by species. Also not reported here are the extensive efforts of the private sector..."*

The Endangered Species Act has become a black hole for taxpayers dollars.

The Pacific Legal Foundation in Sacramento, California related what could be considered a laughable expenditure, were it not so prevalent in our regulatory bureaucracies, who think taxpayers can continually foot all the bills. It seems, in 1994, the US Fish and Wildlife Service gave a $107,000 grant to a consortium of scientists from the University of Washington to study owl droppings. By studying the enzymes and hormones in the droppings, researchers hoped to learn more about the stress levels of owls nesting near logging sites. When do we plug up the black hole?

As economist Milton Friedman once said, "The government solution to a problem is usually as bad as the problem."

The cost of protecting species doesn't stop with the millions of dollars of taxpayers money spent on the extensive recovery plans of the USFWS. Nor does it stop with the millions of dollars in other federal, state, and local expenditures. There is a movement afoot trying to implement an extensive and ambitious plan to protect biodiversity in North America called the Wildlands Project. This plan, first developed and introduced by Earth First! co-founder Dave Foreman, calls for a network of wilderness reserves, human buffer zones, and wildlife corridors stretching across huge tracts of land -- hundreds of millions of acres, as much as half the continent! The Wildlife Project, for example, calls for 23.4 percent of the land on the Oregon coast to be returned to wilderness, and another 26.2 percent to be severely restricted in terms of human use. Most roads would be closed; some would be ripped out of the landscape. That amounts to 49.6 percent of Western Oregon, consisting of federal, state and private property, given over to wilderness with absolutely no plan or concern for the inhabitants. Similar alterations are called for in Vermont, Florida, the mid-Atlantic region, and the rest of the country. One ecologist who helped design this far reaching plan, Reed F. Noss, has said it is a vision of what this continent might look like in 200 years if we can "reduce the scale of human activity". Reduce human activity? To what extent? And at what cost? The frightening thought behind this draconian proposal is that it is gaining support from noted scientists and intellectuals with some influence among the preservationist movement. The $ 13 billion needed by the USFWS, and the $ 300 million plus needed annually by other federal and state agencies, to support the Endangered Species Act as it exists today, would be dwarfed by the social, cultural, and economic costs of this kind of plan. As Dixie Lee Ray would say, "Whatever happened to common sense?"

Private Property Rights

An interesting letter appeared in the *Wall Street Journal* back in May 1992. It was a letter from an out of work logger from Oregon named Donald Walker Jr. He had been out of work since the company he worked for closed down operations in 1989. His wife was able to continue working, but had been transferred to an office 4 hours away, and came home on weekends. In order to survive and supplement their income, Mr. Walker managed his own tree farm that had been in his family for 60 years, harvesting and replanting second growth trees as his father and grandfather before him had done.

Then he received a letter from the lawyers of an outfit called the Forest Conservation Council telling him that if he cut anymore timber on his land, they would sue him for violating the Endangered Species Act, which protects spotted owls (supposedly, whose only habitat is old growth). There had never been a spotted owl on his property as far as he knew, but nonetheless he, along with 200 other small private tree farmers were threatened with extinction. This is not the US Fish and Wildlife Service or the National Marine Fisheries Service regulating thousands of acres of public land under contract with large corporations, but a private self appointed watch dog group of preservationists eroding the private property rights of individuals for their own agenda.

It was suggested by some that Mr. Walker and the others cut down all their trees while they could, before this Forest Conservation Council letter became a court case. He replied, "We don't want to. We're conservationists. This tree farm is our home, and the trees are a part of our way of life. We work with nature to grow a crop the nation needs. The crop is wood. It puts food on the table."

Mr. Walker summed up the situation so aptly by saying, "The problem isn't the owl or even old growth for that matter.

The problem is an out-of-control preservationist movement that doesn't care about people or their rights."

This is just one of many, many examples of the eroding rights of farmers, ranchers, miners, loggers, homeowners, and other private land owners and entrepreneurs. Michael T. Rains, a top US Forest Service official, was quoted as saying, "Public lands will be managed more and more for diversity, and unless private property owners avoid regulation of threatened and endangered species, their private property rights will be eroded.

One third of America's land is already owned by the Federal Government. Public lands comprise about 40 percent of the state of Washington, nearly half of the land in Wyoming, Oregon, and California, 63.8 percent of Idaho, 63.6 percent of Utah, 86.1 percent of Nevada, and nearly 90 percent of Alaska, just to site a few examples. However, for some preservationists and environmental extremists, this is still not enough, and they want to nationalize and lock up more and more private lands.

William Perry Pendley, of the Mountain States Legal Foundation, wrote about a conference in Wyoming in 1992 that was attended by a couple of professors from Rutgers University in New Jersey. They presented a program they called the "Buffalo Commons". Their thesis is that mankind was never meant to live on the Great Plains. This husband-and-wife team named Popper, believe that sooner or later all the people now living in the prairie states will be gone, and that it ought to be sooner. So, the professors have proposed that the US Government "deprivatize" 110 counties in nine states, and move the 400,000 people living there out, so the buffalo can once more roam upon the land.

Far fetched, right? Well, Interior Secretary Bruce Babbitt talks of "discarding the concept of property and trying to find a different understanding of natural landscape." He wants to do away with "the individualistic view of property," and adopt instead a more "communitarian interpretation." This is the head of the Department of the Interior who wants us to rethink the concept of private property.

As Arizona Governor Fife Symington said in 1992, after signing a private property rights bill, "Private property rights lie near the source of the liberty under which Americans are free to enjoy the God-given beauty of the Earth. It is the nature of Government to constantly close in upon that liberty, to diminish it, to consume it. Indeed, one day the historians may put down our era as one where the gradual intrusion of the public upon the private came to deprive Americans of the liberty that was once the envy of most of the world. The right to property is a civil right, no less than the right to freedom of speech and worship, and the rights to due process and equal protection under the law."

We all need to keep in mind the quote by Benjamin Franklin when he said, "Those who are willing to trade a little bit of liberty for a little bit of security, deserve neither."

Agenda

On June 1, 1992, more than 250 of the world's leading scientists, including 27 Nobel laureates, released a statement to the Heads of State attending the United Nations Conference on Environment and Development in Rio de Janeiro. The statement appealed for the use of common sense and reliable science in making recommendations for action on environmental problems. In part the statement says,

> *"We are worried, at the dawn of the 21st century, at the emergence of an irrational ideology which is opposed to scientific and industrial progress and impedes economic and social development...The greatest evils which stalk our Earth are ignorance and oppression, and not Science, Technology, and Industry, whose instruments are indispensable tools of a future shaped by humanity."*

We could certainly use some common sense when it comes to the Endangered Species Act.

What we are seeing, however, is the exact polar positioning by preservationist who are using the Endangered Species Act as a guise to further their own agenda. They continue to use presumptions and hypotheses rather than scientific facts to stifle industrial progress throughout this country.

What exactly is the agenda of the preservationists and the radical environmentalists of the 1990's? As Patrick Moore, one of the original founders of Greenpeace, stated in a speech in 1994, the environmental movement has been split between two factions. Those who advocate a pragmatic approach of working with mainstream business and Government to promote the idea of "sustainable development", where truth mattered and science was respected, and those with more extreme positions in the name of "Deep Ecology", who are calling for a "grassroots revolution against pragmatism and compromise", and taking a "zero-tolerance" and "anti-development" stance at any cost.

Mr. Moore, who left Greenpeace because of their movement toward the latter extremist position, is listed in his former organization's list of anti-environmental organizations, and has been described by Greenpeace as the "eco-Judas". Moore believes this new variant of the environmental movement is so extreme, that its agenda is a greater threat to the global environment than that posed by mainstream society. In looking at what that agenda is, most people would agree.

First, eco-extremism is anti-human. The new extremists characterize the human species as a "cancer" on the face of the earth. All human activity is negative and human intervention is unnatural, when, in fact, we are as much a part of nature and natural evolution as any other species.

Second, it is anti-technology and anti-science. Eco-extremists dream of returning to some kind of technologically primitive society. All large machines are seen as inherently destructive and unnatural,   and "western industrial society" is rejected in its entirety.   The word "nature" is capitalized nearly every time it is used,   and science is invoked only as a means of justifying the adoption of beliefs that have no basis in science to begin with.   One has to wonder how many of these preservationists would be willing to cut their life spans by one half,   see up to half their children die before reaching the age of ten,   live in illiteracy with substandard shelter,   clothing,   and sanitation,   and face bleak prospects of no improvement in economic well-being for themselves or their children.

Furthermore,   the eco-extremists are anti-organization. They expect the whole world to adopt anarchism as the model for individual behavior.   They dislike national Governments,   multi-national corporations and large institutions of all kinds.   All organizations except their own,   that is,   which are large well financed big businesses.

They are anti-trade.   They are not only opposed to "free trade",   but to international trade in general.   They believe that each "bioregion" (the definition of which changes to suit the circumstance) should be self sufficient in all its material needs.   If it's too cold to grow bananas,   too bad.   And yet their actions in litigation behind the Endangered Species Act are making this nation dependent on wood from Indonesia,   New Zealand, and Canada,   beef from Argentina and Australia,   fruits and vegetables from Central and South America,   and oil from the Middle-East.

Preservationists and environmental extremists are anti-free enterprise.   They dislike competition and are definitely opposed to profits.   Anyone engaged in private business,   particularly if they are successful,   is characterized as greedy and lacking in morality. Yet,   what they don't tell us is that the top eleven environmental organizations have combined annual budgets of $ 513.7 million, and the combined salaries of the directors of these organizations is $1,472,761.00!!   Furthermore,   according to the Center for the Defense of Free Enterprise,   almost $ 70 million in taxpayer subsidies have gone to the Nature Conservancy,   the World Wildlife Fund,   Defenders of Wildlife,   and the National Audubon

Society. "These are direct government cash grants paid straight from the United States Treasury into the bank accounts of the eco-groups, not merely tax breaks due to their non-profit status," reports Ron Arnold, executive director for the center. They are continuing this investigation into the top 100 eco-groups, in order to determine the total cost to taxpayers.

Eco-extremism is anti-democratic. This is probably the most dangerous aspect of radical environmentalism. The very foundation of our society, representative democracy, is rejected as being too "human-centered". In the name of "speaking for the trees and other species" we are faced with a movement that would usher in an era of eco-fascism. The "planetary police" would "answer to no one but Mother Earth herself."

And, as Mr. Moore points out, it is anti-civilization. In its very essence, eco-extremism rejects virtually everything about modern society. Nothing short of returning to a primitive tribal society, can save the Earth from ecological collapse. No more cities, no more airplanes, no more wood frame houses, no more supermarkets and no more rights as individuals.

Environmentalism has become a modern religion rather than a matter of science. There is a large gap between the mainstream body of scientific experts and what the public believes, because of the information it gets. The messenger of the preservationists and radical environmentalist movement, the media, is attracted to confrontation and sensation. Many times, advocacy overshadows truth and real news reporting. As Dixie Lee Ray pointed out for instance, Stephen Schneider, a leader of some environmentalists is quoted as saying, "We have to offer up scary scenarios, make simplified, dramatic statements, and make little mention of any doubts we may have. Each of us has to decide what the right balance is between being effective and being honest."

Being effective and being honest! And it is these types of spokespersons who are quoted by the media. Whatever happened to truth in reporting, in objective reporting by the media, and searching for scientific fact? It has given way to advocacy journalism and the public can no longer discern truth from opinion. As David Brooks, an editorial writer for the *Wall Street Journal*, stated, "The reporters who become advocates seem to think they are doing the environment a favor, but it is hard to see how. Because there has been so little critical scrutiny, the politically mainstream environmentalists don't feel compelled to separate themselves from the Greens who think human progress should have stopped in the 19th century."

During a conference of journalists, *Time* science editor Charles Alexander, openly admitted his advocacy toward preservationism. Alexander declared, "As the Science Editor at *Time*, I would freely admit that on this issue we have crossed the boundary from news reporting to advocacy." This from a science editor? A person who is responsible for objectively reporting scientific fact? Where are we to find the truth when our leading news magazines, television, and newspaper journalists "have crossed the boundary from news reporting and advocacy"? And how much can we believe when they have to balance between "being effective and being honest"? They seem to have taken to heart, the tongue-in-cheek philosophy of Mark Twain who said, "Get your facts first, and then you can distort them as much as you please."

An excellent example of this balancing act blew up in the face of the US Fish and Wildlife Service, in a hearing before administrative law judge Harvey Sweitzer. The hearing was to review timber sales in the Oregon coastal range. USFWS contracted to have a video made of spotted owl habitat in the area and present it as evidence in the hearing. However, Judge Sweitzer refused to admit it into evidence after viewing the video himself. It seems that the scenes with owls and owl habitat were shot in Washington's Olympic National Park where federal law prohibits timber harvesting, and on private forest land in the north Cascades hundreds of miles away from the area in question. The balance of effectiveness and honesty was summed up by Judge Sweitzer when he ruled the video be thrown out because of the video's "evidentiary value was substantially outweighed by the danger of unfair prejudice, confusion of the issues, and the possibility of misleading the determination." Interestingly enough, the USFWS has sent this same misleading video to television stations around the country, perpetuating the myth about spotted owl habitat.

Thomas Jefferson once said, "Advertisements contain the only truths to be relied on in the newspaper." It seems he was not only speaking about the press of the 1700's, but was predicting the news worthiness of the media in the 1990's.

Using false, misleading, and prejudicial arguments as scientific fact is what the eco-extremists are doing under the auspices of the Endangered Species Act. Their agenda to stop all development, logging, farming, mining, ranching and economic growth is summed up in the words of Paul Erlich, whose apocalyptic predictions of mass global starvation never come true, who said, "We've already had too much economic growth in the United States...Economic growth in rich countries like ours is the disease, not the cure." And they are using millions of taxpayers dollars to cultivate and culminate this agenda. Environmental groups around the country admit to using the Endangered Species Act as a surrogate reason for slowing down or halting timber cutting as well as mining, grazing, and development on both public and private land. Randall O'Toole of Portland, Oregon, who describes himself as an "eco-activist", is quoted in the September 30, 1991, issue of *Newsweek* as saying, "Cumulatively, the environmental movement is interested in shutting down the timber industry." Period. And a former attorney for the Sierra Club Legal Defense Fund told a group of Women in Timber in California, that he was glad the spotted owl was listed as threatened under the ESA the first time around, but assured them that they had 450 additional species to try if the listing had failed. Preservationists are using the red-cockaded woodpecker in the Southeast to halt logging in that region, the Desert Tortoise is being used to halt grazing rights to cattlemen and woolgrowers as well as mining and development in the Southwest, and they are using other species under the ESA to stop multiple-use of all public lands and commercial use of private lands.

What is good for the goose, however, may not always be good for the gander. The Sierra Club along with seven other environmental groups is suing the Forest Service for "bad management" of the Colville National Forest in Washington. The Northwest regional Director of the Sierra Club, William Arthur, who has 42 acres near the Colville National Forest and bordered on three sides by the Little Pend Oreille Wildlife Recreation Area, however, feels his management practices of land are different. Allen decided to clear-cut 80-90 percent of the trees on his property among which was a 270 year old cedar.

And Jon Roush, president of the Wilderness Society logged 400,000 board feet of timber off his Bitterroot Valley, Montana ranch. This was after blocking a timber sale on the property next to his saying the sale would harm stream and wildlife. His reasoning for this cut was that he needed the money for a divorce settlement, even though he has a $2 million ranch and makes in excess of $120,000 per year. Journalist Alexander Cockburn, in an article about the timber sale in *Nation* magazine, writes, "The head of the Wilderness Society logging old growth in the Bitterroot Valley is roughly akin to the head of Human Rights Watch torturing a domestic servant."

Some mainstream environmentalist, however, feel that the time has come for compromise. To use common sense and put the human element back into the environmental equation. After all, ecology and economy are both derived from the same Greek word *oikos*, which means "house of living relations." Man is part of nature, and our economy is part of our ecology.

National Audubon Society's Brock Evans is quoted in *US News* as saying, "We were on a crusade for righteousness and good, out to save the world. Our intentions were high, we felt we were doing the right thing, but we were insensitive." He went on to say it was easy for environmentalists to dismiss farmers, ranchers, land owners, and timber workers while inflexible, expensive green laws were creating financial hardships and eliminating jobs.   "All these people could have been our allies", Evans said, "but we ignored them." Evans realized that all of the people he was talking about -- those that work with the land -- are the true conservationists.

However,   as the mainstream environmentalists move toward compromise and common sense, the preservationist-eco-extremist fringe is mounting an ever increasing assault on business, free enterprise, and private property rights. And they are using the Endangered Species Act to that end.   The only limitations facing them are the number of lawyers they can afford on their multi-million dollar budgets.

Solutions

In a recent US Supreme Court decision regarding the Endangered Species Act, the Court reversed an appeals court decision and said the Federal Government can regulate private land to protect endangered species.   The decision in Babbitt v Sweet Home, went against the basic premise of the original act, and has opened a Pandora's box that will have a legislative backlash in an attempt to bring common sense back into the law. Unfortunately, because of the far reaching implications of this decision, the pendulum might swing even farther from what is necessary to both save species and protect personal property rights and economic sustainability.   In this case,   threatened species will probably loose out. Why?

The authors of the original Endangered Species Act of 1973, a unanimous bi-partisan group of legislators from both sides of the Hill, specifically intended that the Act was to have regulatory authority over federal lands only. They believed in the 5th Amendment of the Constitution of the United States that specifically protects private property from Government intervention.   It was also abundantly clear in the wording and intent, that the Act regulated direct harm to a species, such as hunting, trapping,   or killing.   It did not extend the same regulatory clout to species habitat that might be used by a passing specie on private land. The federal appeals court agreed, but in a 6-3 decision, the Supreme Court reversed their decision. As Justice Antonin Scalia said in a dissenting opinion, " to extend protection to habitat imposed unfairness to the point of financial ruin -- not just to the rich, but upon the simplest farmer who finds his land conscripted to national zoological use." And although this decision involved the spotted owl, it has much wider implications. If it applies to one species anywhere, it applies to all species everywhere.

The Act's implementation has been pursued with reckless abandon throughout the nation, not just in the Pacific Northwest. Farmers', ranchers', loggers', and miners' attempts to provide food, fiber, timber, and minerals, are being slowed and halted to save endangered species. Reasonable implementation of the Endangered Species Act calls for balancing environmental quality with the economic livelihood and cultural identity of all communities.

First and foremost, the Endangered Species Act must be implemented with the basic premise of the 5th amendment at its core. Government agencies have shifted their regulatory direction following the lead of William Reilly, who as head of the Environmental Protection Agency in 1991, called private ownership of land a "quaint anachronism." He, and others, have called for the repeal of the Fifth Amendment to make it easier for the Government to seize private land. He has stated, "a mere loss in land value is no justification for invalidating the regulation of land use." Facist, Communist, and Nazi leaders of the world, in this century, have made similar, and even less constricting, diatribes.

The Fifth Amendment says in part, No person shall...be deprived of life, liberty or property, without due process of law; nor shall private property be taken for public use without just compensation. So, the number one priority in the implementation of the Endangered Species Act, should be to put the Constitution back into the act. Work with private land owners, offering economic incentives, to encourage land management which takes into consideration wildlife and wildlife habitat. And, to insure that in so doing, future restrictions are not meted out because a land owner has created a "new habitat." The story of the wood duck is a true success story of volunteerism, which worked to bring an almost extinct species, to the second most common duck today. "Friends of the Wood Duck", farmers, ranchers and hunters, at the turn of the century, built and installed hundreds of thousands of wood duck boxes on their own land, and voluntarily protected and encouraged the proliferation of the species, until it became plentiful. Today, if a land owner sets aside a percentage of their land for habitat for the spotted owl, Texas salamander, or red-cockaded woodpecker, the rest of his property is in jeopardy of being restricted for use under the Endangered Species Act. Where is the incentive to protect species on private land?

One of the primary target industries of the preservationists movement, is the much maligned timber industry. The preservationists are capable of playing on the emotions of an ill-informed (or in many cases a misinformed) public regarding both public and private forest lands. The constant barrage of plea letters and thirty-second sound bites in the media, recounting the total destruction of our forests, the greenhouse effect, and the annihilation of the last of the rain forests, does nothing to relate the truth, but people line up with their wallets out to feed the litany of lawyers who continuously file lawsuits in the name of the ESA.

It doesn't matter that there is two-thirds as much forest land in this nation today as there was in 1600. This in spite of the conversion of 370 million acres of forest land to other uses, principally agriculture. Add to this the enormous harvest that has been necessary to build the nation's homes, warm its citizens and fuel its early-day engines. And to this total, add all the losses to forest fires, diseases and insect infestations, and even after all of this, the nation still has two-thirds as much forest land as was here when the pilgrims landed.

Calvin and Hobbes

by Bill Watterson

Nor does it matter to the preservationists that there are more trees growing in America's forest today than any time since the early 1900's, and that forest growth exceeds harvest by 37%. Furthermore, 70% of America's national forest land base is in land use categories where timber production is forbidden.

It doesn't matter to preservationists, but it makes for emotional fodder to stir up the people who have never seen a national forest or know the facts about sustained harvesting or forest management. Most people in this country have never even seen an old growth forest or a commercial tree farm, and couldn't tell the difference between a 200 year old fir and an 80 year old pine. And yet they feel like they can dictate the land management practices, and biological management practices, in the Pacific North West or the forests of the South East from the plains of Iowa and the halls of Washington, DC

Michael Mann, director of the movie "Last of the Mohicans", searched nation wide for an old growth forest that would depict the untouched 18th century landscape of upstate New York. What he found that represented old growth and finally decided to use was a 12,000 acre forest surrounding Lake James in North Carolina, just 75 miles from Charlotte.

What Mann didn't realize was that the oldest tree on the site was only 30 years old. The pines nearest the fort built for the movie set were only 19 years old. George Moyers, who manages the forest for Crescent Resources, said the land had previously been clearcut and replanted. In about 20 years, the property will be clearcut and replanted again. Needless to say, the film crew was taken aback at the discovery that they were using a young growth forest.

It is necessary that we use scientific fact and scientific management as critical factors in the implementation of the Endangered Species Act. Furthermore, implementation of the ESA needs to be placed in the hands of local scientific managers that can make decisions based on the needs of the local communities as well as the biological needs of the forest.

The Endangered Species Act is a lawyer's Full Employment Act. Lawyers Vic Sher and Todd True, of the Sierra Club Legal Defense Fund in the Pacific Northwest, have stated that in order to accomplish their agenda, "it would take a coordinated effort, a coordinated series of lawsuits."

An example of these "series of lawsuits" was made evident in the Siskiyou National Forest, where only 37% of the forest is available for timber production. The US Forest service has developed and introduced what they call a new perspective in forestry, which balances timber production and forest preservation through a scientifically-based management strategy. According to the project leader, Kurt Wiedenmann, "The only thing we could do to further minimize risks associated with road construction and harvesting is do nothing at all". Apparently, preservationists feel that doing nothing is the way to go, since they promised to sue the Forest Service, no matter what the Environmental Impact Statement said or what the final plan proposed. After Congress passed a bill restricting frivolous lawsuits affecting the forest management plan of the Siskiyou National Forest, logging was resumed. Less than one-third of the timber in the designated logging area was harvested, no roads were built, and all timber was removed by helicopter, in order to have a minimum effect on the environment. However, this was still not enough for some preservationist, and representatives from the National Audubon Society, Sierra Club, Earth First! and other preservationists groups tried to block the approved logging show.

The trend with these demonstrations and frivolous lawsuits is to block all extractive industries from public lands. This means no forestry, no mining, no grazing, no oil and gas exploration, and no development of water resources. And the mere threat of lawsuits has been affective to halt the Forest Service to uphold their legal commitment to multiple use management. All industries dependent on natural resources that have been available on public lands are going to be left out in the cold. There isn't a resource-based industry in America that is free from the threat from preservationists, or affected by the Endangered Species Act.

The time has come to limit frivolous lawsuits aimed at crippling the economic development of local communities, and return the management of public lands back to the professionals to manage them for multiple use. When forests are not allowed to be managed properly, insect infestations, wide spread disease, and out of control forest fires wipe out our precious natural resources, and wildlife, local communities, and our nation as a whole end up the losers.

Tragedies often are caused by haphazard regulations, as was the case in 1994 when wild fires wiped out 3.3 million acres nationwide. Fourteen firefighters were killed battling Western US forest fires, and the mismanagement of the forests in the name of endangered species was a major contributing factor. A National Forest Policy that puts a premium on preservation and discourages management, even for safety, has kept National Forests throughout the US from their traditional harvests of diseased and weak stands of timber and fire-spreading underbrush. And those fourteen firefighters paid the ultimate price.

National Forests and the timber industry are not the only targets of the preservationist movement, nor the only ones affected by the misuse of the Endangered Species Act. Private property owners, farmers, ranchers, fishermen, miners, builders, developers and those commercially or socially connected to them, are affected. It constantly intrudes on their lives, challenges their fundamental rights, and even threatens their livelihoods.

The truth is that all Americans, whether or not they think twice about endangered species, are in one way or another directly affected by them, even if there isn't one living in their backyard. We all pay the bills for the actions our Government takes, and we pick up the tab when government regulations increase the cost of consumer goods. We also feel its effects indirectly, when the money spent on endangered species is not available for other things such as education, housing, or health care.

It doesn't matter whether you live in Oregon, Alabama, or Ohio, officially listed endangered species can be found in every state, and more will be added as time goes by. The Endangered Species Act is simply the most far-reaching and powerful environmental law in history. It can affect you if you own or plan to own property, if you want to build on or otherwise improve your property, if you like to hunt or fish, if you enjoy hiking, camping, or even mountain biking.

Most Americans would support the protection of threatened and endangered species. Society has an important and vital obligation to conserve our natural resources (including threatened and endangered species) in a responsible and intelligent manner. But the crux is "responsible and intelligent". The plain truth is that protecting the environment, fostering free market enterprise, and preserving private property rights are inextricably connected concepts that work together to enhance environmental quality. Being connected means that private stewardship of natural resources is a means of ensuring "sustainability". If we take away the incentive to manage private resources for the future, by punishing land owners for creating or developing habitat, we will no longer have habitat on private property.

So economic incentives need to be addressed in the implementation of the Endangered Species Act. Interior Secretary Bruce Babbitt has proposed changes in administrative policy that are supposed to make the act more "user friendly". One such change is that social and economic impacts resulting from implementing a recovery plan be "minimized". This needs to be more than just an administrative policy change, and needs to more than just "minimize" economic impact, but it is a start.

A positive example of how Government can work with private property owners for the protection and recovery of endangered species, shows up in North Carolina in a program called "Safe Harbor". Pinehurst Resort and Country Club in

North Carolina was the first participant in an Interior Department program that encourages development of habitat for endangered species by promising exemptions from land-use restrictions in the future. The club, home to the red-cockaded woodpecker, will make habitat improvements such as clearing hardwood undergrowth trees, not do any development during nesting seasons, and work with Fish and Wildlife in relocation projects when necessary. In other words, manage their property in a species-friendly way, with the promise that the Government will not come along down the road and say this property is prime habitat, and cannot be touched by human hands.

Another similar success story of a government agency working with private landowners to benefit endangered species, also comes from the Southeast US. Westvaco Corp., a timber company that has had a woodpecker protection plan since 1971 (two years before the Endangered Species Act), and the US Fish and Wildlife Service have worked out a pact to protect the red-cockaded woodpecker on Westvaco land. The agreement is called the "first of its kind", and the goal is to maintain the bird's genetic diversity and to expand populations in suitable habitat. USFWS biologists and Westvaco staff trap young red-cockaded woodpeckers in isolated clusters on company land, and surplus juveniles in other clusters. The birds are then moved to public forests that are part of the woodpecker recovery program. By moving birds from isolated clusters into existing recovery populations, the rate of population growth increases. Suitable forest habitat for the woodpecker in the thirteen southeastern states where it lives totals 4 million acres, 80% of which is federal land. Relocation on to federal land is a win-win situation.

These are only two examples of the positive solutions that can be accomplished when a government agency uses common sense to resolve a critical issue. We hope there are others. All too often, however, we hear of government agencies as adversaries rather than allies to common sense. For example, when fourteen-year-old Boy Scout Robert Graham got lost in a Wilderness area of the Santa Fe National Forest, he was spotted by a helicopter two days later. The Forest Service, however, refused to let the helicopter land to retrieve Graham because of the area's Wilderness designation which forbids motorized vehicles of any kind in the forest. The Forest Service finally relented and allowed the helicopter to land and rescue the boy, who had been lost in the wild for three days.

Then there was the story of the man from Port Bolivar, Texas who was forced by the Environmental Protection Agency and the Army Corps of Engineers to post in front of his home a 10-foot-high, 20-foot-wide sign describing his transgression of depositing "illegal fill material" on his property, deemed a wetland. The sign, like an enormous Scarlet Letter of shame, names the man twice, notes that he must remove the filler at his own expense, re-vegetate the wetlands, pay civil penalties, and foot the bill for restoration of the property.

This certainly must pertain to a commercial development of some "unscrupulous major developer", right? Wrong. This property, on the Gulf Coast of Texas, is less than one half acre, is located just fifty feet from a major highway, and has been owned by the man for 20 years. It was the site of a muddy bait camp with outdoor latrines and hardly regarded as an ecologically valuable wetlands, and all the man wanted to do was build his retirement home. On less than one half acre.

We need to build common sense back into the environmental equation in general, and the Endangered Species Act in particular. One of the arguments for keeping the ESA intact as it now stands, is that "medical marvels" are derived from living things that will all go extinct if not protected. Doctors say that nearly one-quarter of prescriptions written in the United States today are based on substances derived from natural products. We have vincristine for treating leukemia that came from the rosy periwinkle; taxol used in treating ovarian and breast cancer from the bark of the Pacific yew tree; digitalis from purple foxglove; an anti-inflammatory antihistamine comes from the wheat fungus ergot; and the Australian mulberry tree and the

Cameroon vine tree are said to produce AIDS-fighting compounds.

Yet, according to Tom Eisner, a Cornell University biology professor, less than 5% of the flowering plants that exist today have been studied for their chemical make-up. It seems to make more sense to spend the time and money studying ways to reproduce what we have in the way of plants and animals and finding ways to become more productive in their propagation and population growth, rather than lock up public and private land in the name of the environment, and using the ESA to that means.

It is time for Congressional members and environmental lobbyists to face reality. They can no longer claim that "the act works, for people as well as for animals and plants", as the president of The Nature Conservancy asserted in *The Wall Street Journal*. It doesn't. The ESA has costs -- economic, constitutional, and environmental. It would be a tragedy if, because of wasteful, inefficient, inaffective, and out of touch government regulations, the public support of endangered species is eroded. It is time to follow some of the suggestions listed here, as a starting point for intelligent and productive management of endangered species to ensure a better future for both humans and our nations species.

Politicians must understand that if they want to use private property as public wildlife refuges, then they must abide by the Fifth Amendment of the Constitution and compensate the owners for such public uses.

Implementation of the Endangered Species Act must take into consideration the economic and social impact of local communities and individuals.

Listing of species has to take into consideration scientific fact and genetical commonality of species, rather than every local population for political or personal agendas.

There must be an end to frivolous lawsuits that cost millions of taxpayer dollars and have legitimate government agencies that by law are committed to multiple use, doing nothing for fear of litigation.

We must allow professional, scientific management of our public lands to ensure continued health of our forests, animal habitats, and economic stability of our nation.

Use budgeted and allocated funds to research reproduction, relocation and propagation of endangered plants and animals.

Encourage voluntary habitat development and species protection, with legal protection from future land-use restrictions, as well as with economic incentives.

As currently written, and interpreted by the courts, the Endangered Species Act lacks the flexibility to balance human needs with the needs of other species. There has to be a balance that preserves mankind's place in nature, and the only way to assure that balance is by better understanding how laws to protect "nature" can affect mankind. And when a law, as Randy Fitzgerald wrote in Reader's Digest, goes "haywire", or when we have to ask ourselves, as Dixie Lee Ray asked, "What ever happened to common sense", then its time to make changes and adjustments to get the balance back.

CHEF'S DRY MEASURES

$$1 \text{ cup} = 8 \text{ fl oz} = 16 \text{ Tbsp} = 48 \text{ tsp} = 237 \text{ ml}$$

$$\tfrac{3}{4} \text{ cup} = 6 \text{ fl oz} = 12 \text{ Tbsp} = 36 \text{ tsp} = 177 \text{ ml}$$

$$\tfrac{2}{3} \text{ cup} = 5\tfrac{1}{3} \text{ fl oz} = 10\tfrac{2}{3} \text{ Tbsp} = 32 \text{ tsp} = 158 \text{ ml}$$

$$\tfrac{1}{2} \text{ cup} = 4 \text{ fl oz} = 8 \text{ Tbsp} = 24 \text{ tsp} = 118 \text{ ml}$$

$$\tfrac{1}{3} \text{ cup} = 2\tfrac{2}{3} \text{ fl oz} = 5\tfrac{1}{3} \text{ Tbsp} = 16 \text{ tsp} = 79 \text{ ml}$$

$$\tfrac{1}{4} \text{ cup} = 2 \text{ fl oz} = 4 \text{ Tbsp} = 12 \text{ tsp} = 59 \text{ ml}$$

$$\tfrac{1}{8} \text{ cup} = 1 \text{ fl oz} = 2 \text{ Tbsp} = 6 \text{ tsp} = 30 \text{ ml}$$

$$1 \text{ Tbsp} = 3 \text{ tsp} = 15 \text{ ml}$$

CHEF'S LIQUID MEASURES

$$1 \text{ gal} = 4 \text{ qt} = 8 \text{ pt} = 16 \text{ cup} = 128 \text{ fl oz} = 3.79 \text{ L}$$

$$\tfrac{1}{2} \text{ gal} = 2 \text{ qt} = 4 \text{ pt} = 8 \text{ cup} = 64 \text{ fl oz} = 1.89 \text{ L}$$

$$\tfrac{1}{4} \text{ gal} = 1 \text{ qt} = 2 \text{ pt} = 4 \text{ cup} = 32 \text{ fl oz} = .95 \text{ L}$$

$$\tfrac{1}{2} \text{ qt} = 1 \text{ pt} = 2 \text{ cup} = 16 \text{ fl oz} = .47 \text{ L}$$

$$\tfrac{1}{4} \text{ qt} = \tfrac{1}{2} \text{ pt} = 1 \text{ cup} = 8 \text{ fl oz} = .24 \text{ L}$$

$$\tfrac{1}{8} \text{ qt} = \tfrac{1}{4} \text{ pt} = \tfrac{1}{2} \text{ cup} = 4 \text{ fl oz} = .12 \text{ L}$$

RECIPES

As I have stated throughout this book, nobody is against saving truly endangered species, and as the law was originally written and intended, I certainly would not advocate harassing, pursuing, hunting, shooting, wounding, killing, trapping, capturing or collecting endangered species. However, when preservationist groups continually promote misinformation such as "the law works for people, as well as animals", and the absurd contention that the World Wildlife Fund espouses, that "without firing a shot, we may kill one-fifth of all species of life on this planet in the next ten years", it is time to balance absurdity with some levity. For this reason, I have included in this section, a number of rather nonsensical and satirical "recipes" for preparing "endangered species". I don't encourage their use in reality, but rather include them here to show how inane extremism can be.

Preservationists have asserted that currently 27,000 species become extinct every year, and by the year 2000, that figure will become 40,000. They base these unscientific figures on guess work by extrapolating estimated extinction figures from Thomas Lovejoy, who, as a biologist, has admitted were a guess to begin with. These extrapolations, which are determined through a static unchanging set of criteria, are akin to saying that the normal growth rate of a two year old child will inevitably produce a person eight feet tall by the time they are twelve.

There never has been, nor ever will be a static, unchanging environment to profess these ridiculous claims. Enough absurdity.

Furthermore, as you will see in this section, the unfounded and inaccurate claim that the Endangered Species Act is good for people, is just as preposterous. We will look at how individuals, farmers, miners, ranchers, loggers and entire communities have been affected by the Endangered Species Act.

Stephens' Kangaroo Rat
Dipodomys stephensi

The Stephens' kangaroo rat is an example of obscure taxonomy, in that it is a member of the species Dipodomys, but varies from the other kangaroo rats by its geographical location. The Stephens' kangaroo rat is located in Riverside County in Southern California about 80 miles east of Los Angeles, and was listed as an endangered species in 1988. Since that time, the Government has spent about $100 million dollars of taxpayers money to protect it, and have locked up 77,000 acres of private property as a study area. Study areas are strictly "protected".

During October of 1993, the people who live in the study area found out just how inflexible the ESA really is. Wildfires swept through the area burning 25,000 acres and destroying 29 homes. Homeowners like Yshmael Garcia and Anna Klimko lost their homes, as a direct result of not being able to disc a fire break around them. The Riverside County Fire District ordered homeowners, well before the fire season, to "abate the flammable vegetation" around their homes, which they were eager to do. However, US Fish and Wildlife Services warned the homeowners in a letter that "discing of the firebreak would harm" the kangaroo rat, and thus "is not authorized" by the Endangered Species Act. FWS went on to say, "It should be noted that the Act provides for both criminal and civil penalties" for discing -- in this case going to federal prison or being fined up to $100,000.   Those homeowners that went ahead and disced fire breaks were spared the disaster of total loss.

Interior Secretary, Bruce Babbitt, told the media after the fires, "the lesson of these fires is that we've got to keep the people away from the fire hazard." Apparently, keeping the fire hazard away from people was not worth considering.

ROAST KANGAROO RAT A LA RIVERSIDE

Kangaroo rat meat is tender and soft. The animal has kernels or scent glands that are found between the forelegs, under the thighs and along the spine in the small of the back. They should be removed immediately after the skin has been removed, taking care not to cut into them. One way to make kangaroo rat more mild in flavor is to cover it with boiling water and add 1 tablespoon each of baking soda and black pepper, then simmer for ten to fifteen minutes, drain and cook in the usual way.

4-6 Stephens' kangaroo rats
Baking soda
Salt
Sliced onions
Strips of bacon

Remove all surface fat from the rats. Cover meat with a weak solution of soda and water (1 teaspoon soda to 1 quart of water). Parboil by simmering gently for 10 minutes. Drain, place meat in roaster, sprinkle with salt, cover with sliced onions, strips of bacon, and roast in moderate oven (350° F.) until well done. Serve at once. Kangaroo rat should be cooked until the meat almost falls off the bones.

Suggested Wine: Sauvignon Blanc

Discing fire breaks is not the only restriction in what is called the K-rat study area. In 1991, Michael Rowe, his wife and three children moved into a small one-bedroom home on their 20-acre hilltop ranch. That same year, after saving enough money to expand their house, Mr. Rowe was told that his ranch was part of the K-rat study area, and was denied permission to build. He was told that if he came up with $5,000 to hire a biologist, he might be allowed the use of his land. If a biological survey found no kangaroo rats on his land, he could use the property after paying $1,950 an acre in "development mitigation fees" (to subsidize the purchase of occupied habitat elsewhere). However, if one single rat were found on his property, even this would be negated.

Mr. Rowe, like many others, wonders, "By what authority do these do-gooders, with their tract homes and condos that destroyed prior habitat, determine that my property should remain open space for them to have hills to look at?" He notes that "not one of the advocates for preservation of the K-rats owns property in the designated habitat preserves." His suggestion: "Let them bring their checkbooks, purchase the property and they can look at it all they want."

COOPER'S ENTRECOTE

There are many kinds of rats and mice in various parts of the world. In fact, over a quarter of all species of mammals are rats and ratlike rodents. All of them are no doubt edible, and a few are eaten on a regular basis.

Before mechanical refrigeration was invented, rats were often eaten aboard ships, and were purchased at exorbitant prices from the ship's ratcatcher. They have also been skinned and sold as black-market squirrels. Even today rats are popular in parts of China, and are even served in a Canton restaurant, which prepares them in 17 ways, including "golden rat."   ☞

G. Gordon Liddy said that he ate a rat --
fried the American way. Also, Henry David
Thoreau is reported to have said that he enjoyed
fried rats, served with a little relish.

During the siege of Paris in 1870, the French
coopers skinned rats, marinated them in a mixture
of olive oil and chopped shallots, and then grilled
them whole over fires made with the wood from
broken-up wine barrels. Called Cooper's Entrecote,
it was a forerunner of other grilled French dishes.

In 1990 nearly half of the 3,200-acre farm owned by the
Domenigoni family was placed in a habitat preserve study area
without the family's knowledge. The family had farmed the land
since 1879, producing cattle, alfalfa, wheat, barley and other
grains. Biologists, hired by the Riverside Habitat Conservation
Agency, were discovered trespassing on the Domenigoni land
collecting information on the Stephens' kangaroo rat. A month
later Domenigoni decided to plant a grain crop and when he
prepared to disc 800 acres of the land that had been lying fallow
due to a drought, he was told by US Fish and Wildlife personnel
he would be arrested for "taking" the K-rats that occupied the
area. He was also told he would be subject to penalties of the
ESA, which included impoundment of his farm equipment and a
year in jail, a $50,000 fine, or both. They also have been
prevented from cutting fire breaks to protect neighbors' homes
from the fire danger created by overgrown weeds on the
property. The field has been idled for five crop years at an
uncompensated loss of income of $75,000 a year.

STEPHEN'S KANGAROO RAT TACO

6-8 dressed k-rats	1 head lettuce
2 firm tomatoes	$\frac{1}{4}$ lb. cheddar
$\frac{1}{4}$ lb. pepper jack cheese	cheese
1 onion, chopped finely	Medium hot peppers
$\frac{1}{2}$ cup salsa	$\frac{1}{2}$ cup green taco
$\frac{1}{2}$ cup red taco sauce	sauce
8 corn tortillas	2 T peanut oil

Cut Kangaroo rat into small pieces. Brown in non-stick pan, and drain fat. Add salsa and taco sauces and simmer over low heat for 20 minutes. In meantime, chop lettuce, tomatoes, peppers, and onion, and grate cheese. Set aside in separate bowls or "Lazy Susan".

Heat tortillas in 1 tablespoon of peanut oil for each 4 tortillas, and set aside on paper towels. Place in oven with only pilot to keep warm.

Serve tortillas with 1 tablespoon of each ingredient and wrap ends. Adjust mix of ingredients per personal taste. Serves 4.

Suggested beverage: Mexican beer and shot of Tequila.

Another couple learned that their 900 acres of land had been placed in a habitat preserve study area when they attempted to get permits to install two mobilehomes. They had intended to raise citrus and subtropical fruit in the unique climate. An attempt to get the property removed from the preserve took 18 months and was denied by the FWS. They were told their property was needed as a corridor linking a kangaroo rat preserve with the Cleveland National Forest even though Interstate 15 lies between their property and the national forest. They have yet to receive any compensation for loss in value and use of their own land.

A native American Indian from the Cahuilla tribe in southern Riverside County raises cattle to feed his family and supplement his income from an auto repair job. To feed the cattle, he raises oat hay on land he leases from the tribe. In November, 1992 a tractor operator he hired to disc the land for planting was confronted by a US Fish and Wildlife biologist who ordered him to immediately stop discing or risk being arrested and having his tractor impounded. The threats and intimidation were enough to stop the planting and the native American had to purchase hay to feed his cattle. He still has not been compensated for the hay he had to buy.

The Los Angeles Water Department finished a 4,500-foot-long "K-rat wall" in 1991, built at a cost of $360,000. The two-foot high barrier is to stop kangaroo rats from hopping into a filtration plant. The penalty for killing a K-rat can be $50,000 and a year in jail.

Tipton Kangaroo Rat
Dipodomys nitratoides nitratoides

Another K-rat, only this one is found in the agriculturally rich San Joaquin Valley of central California. Agriculture, as well as logging, mining and ranching, is a primary target of preservationists groups who use the ESA to intimidate, regulate and legislate, to try and stop economic growth and development. And with the Tipton kangaroo rat, the Government seems to have attacked with both barrels.

Taung Ming-Lin, a Chinese immigrant, bought 723 acres of farm land in Kern County, California, with the intention of growing bamboo sprouts and other Chinese vegetables to sell to Asian communities in southern California. After discing his property in preparation for planting, Ming-Lin was cited by US Fish and Wildlife Services for altering the habitat of the Tipton kangaroo rat, and for "taking" an endangered species when he allegedly ran over one of the K-rats. The charges carry a one year prison term and up to $300,000 in fines, not to mention the cost of defending himself in federal court. Ming-Lin, who does not speak English, has said through an interpreter, that he had no knowledge of the K-rat, and was told by County officials that the land was zoned for farming and he did not need a permit to plow his own fields.

FARLEY'S CREAMED TIPTON K-RAT
(Adapted from Farley Mowat's *Never Cry Wolf*)

1 dozen k-rats	salt and pepper
1 cup white flour	cloves
1 piece sowbelly (or salt pork)	ethyl alcohol

Skin and dress the k-rats, but do not remove the heads. Wash, then place in a pot with enough alcohol to cover the carcasses. Allow to marinate for about two hours. Cut sowbelly into small cubes and fry slowly until most of the fat has been rendered. Remove the k-rats from the alcohol and roll them in a mixture of salt, pepper and flour. Place in large frying pan and sauté for about five minutes (being careful not to allow the pan to get too hot, or the delicate meat will dry out and become tough and stringy). Add a cup of alcohol and six or eight cloves. Cover the pan and allow to simmer slowly for fifteen minutes.   ☞

Make a cream sauce according to any standard recipe. When the sauce is ready, drench the carcasses with it, cover and allow to rest in a warm place for ten minutes before serving.

Suggested Beverage: Three fingers of Jack Daniels

Other farms in the San Joaquin Valley have also been targets of the ESA. A farm near the city of Bakersfield, California which irrigates with wastewater from the city was charged with 12 counts of disturbing the habitat of endangered species and faced possible fines of $300,000. A spokesman for the City of Bakersfield said, "We have to have somewhere to spread the water. This situation could have disastrous consequences for the city." This could have even farther reaching consequences as cities throughout the country are studying ways to deal with their reclaimed waste water. Of course in this instance, according to the farmer, he could continue to operate on his land if he would give the state 640 acres of his land and a $300,000 "fee".

Some possible substitutions: Amargosa vole, Fresno kangaroo rat, Giant kangaroo rat, Hualapai Mexican vole, Key Largo woodrat, Merriam's kangaroo rat, Morro Bay kangaroo rat, Rice rat.

Kanab Amber Snail
Oxyloma haydeny kanabensis

A retired construction industry worker and his wife, Brandt and Venice Child, moved to Kane County, Utah, and bought 500 acres of land in Three Lakes, Utah. They purchased $75,000 worth of heavy equipment, and began work on a recreational park, campground and golf course around the three lakes on their property. The area had been used by the people of southern Utah as a recreation area for years, and Child's land was ideal for the planned improvements. Shortly after he began work on his property, the Fish and Wildlife Service informed Child that the three aquifer-fed ponds on his land were inhabited by 200,000 endangered thumbnail-sized Kanab ambersnails. The area was fenced off, people were no longer allowed on the ponds' banks, and Child was forbidden to work in the area. He estimates his losses at $2.5 million. When Child objected to this intrusion upon his property and said, "This is my land; I own it and I pay taxes on it," a Government agent responded, "You may own it and you may pay taxes on it, but we control it."

STUFFED KANAB AMBERSNAILS

To prepare fresh snails, soak live snails in salt water 5 hours. Wash and rinse several times. Boil 30 minutes. Pick snails from shells and boil in fish stock (Gila trout, Colorado squawfish, or Bonytail chub) 3 to 4 hours.

50 or so snails	1 T chopped celery
50 or so shells	1 t chopped onion
2 T butter	$\frac{1}{8}$ t pepper
2 T chopped parsley	

Force snails into shells. Pack opening with a mixture of the other ingredients. Bake in a moderate oven (350° F) 30 minutes. Serve hot. Serves 6.

Wine Suggestion: Chardonnay

To add insult to injury, Child notified Fish and Wildlife when a flock of 10 domestic geese took up residence at his ponds. He new that if he did not report a problem, he could be held accountable, and if any of the geese ate any of the snails, the owner could face a $50,000 fine for each snail. Fish and Wildlife then requested the Utah Department of Wildlife and Resources to send someone to shoot the geese, remove their stomachs and bring the contents to Salt Lake City so they could determine how many snails had been eaten. When a state wildlife agent and a Highway Patrolman arrived, however, they were confronted by Jeanie Hunt, a reporter for the *Southern Utah News* and told them that she would take pictures. Ms. Hunt said they backed off saying it would be bad PR if the agency was portrayed as killing innocent geese to save a few snails. As an alternate plan, the Fish and Wildlife Service (although they deny it) derived a plan to induce vomiting in the geese and analyzing the contents. When analyzed, however, the vomit contained no snails. In any case, today, the geese are living elsewhere, the snail population thrives in the ponds, and Mr. Child has never been compensated for the loss of his property.

Bruneau Hot Springsnail
Pyrgulopsis bruneauansis

      The Bruneau hot springsnail was listed as an endangered species in 1993 and effectively shut down agriculture in the Bruneau Valley of Idaho. The Farmers Home Administration received a consultation letter from the Fish and Wildlife Service on April 26, 1993 stating that no FmHA operating loans would be granted to farmers and ranchers in the area after 1993, because spring discharge of the water from Hot Creek would adversely affect the springsnail habitat. As a result, local banks were requiring a two-year guarantee for the irrigation water required for each operator prior to granting any loans. Bank loans are at a higher cost, harder to get and require considerably more restrictions.

      The Bruneau Hot Springsnail, about the size of this comma, was said to be found in only three colonies near the Snake River in the Bruneau Valley. After listing the snail on the endangered list, the US Fish and Wildlife Service moved to cut off 59 farms and ranches from their water rights to avoid lowering the water level of the hot springs where the snails are found. Farmers and ranchers in this agricultural valley think it is ludicrous to worry about a snail that is so prolific that it can be found in concentrations of 6,000 snails per square foot. Furthermore, an additional 125 colonies of snails have been found in the area, a far cry from the three listed by the Fish and Wildlife Service.

SNAKE RIVER SALMON BAIT

The Bruneau hot springsnail is so small, trying to even handle one at a time proves to be impossible. How biologists determined that the only distinguishable trait of this tiny creature is its proportionately large sex organ, is beyond me. However, given the fact that it takes thousands to cover a regular dinner plate, the best possible use for these snails is as bait, in a mixture of corn meal and roe. Coho, Sockeye, Snake River and Chinook salmon love the concoction, and those not actually landed are certainly fattened by these tiny morsels.

In December of 1993, Federal Judge Harold Ryan removed the tiny Idaho snail from the Endangered Species list after a lawsuit by the 100 or so farmers and ranchers in the affected area. He chastised the US Fish and Wildlife Service for withholding scientific data from the public and said its behavior represented "self-serving and superficial responses" from an agency that had already made up its mind. Although it looks like the people of the Bruneau Valley may survive this ordeal, it is just another example of how the Endangered Species Act is misused by extremists in the BANANA movement: Build Absolutely Nothing Anywhere Near Anything.

Some possible substitutions: Alamosa springsnail, Chittenango ovate amber snail, Flat-spired snail, Iowa pleistocene snail, Noonday snail, Oahu tree snail, Painted snake coiled forest snail, Socorro springsnail, Tulotoma snail, Utah valvata snail, or any of the additional 25 snails proposed for listing.

Puritan Tiger Beetle
Cicindela puritana

As Harvard professor E.O. Wilson said, "God seems to have had a fondness for beetles." The National Wilderness Institute estimates the world holds in excess of 290,000 species of beetles with more than 28,600 in North America. The puritan tiger beetle is one of about 130 or so North American species belonging to the genus *Cicindela*. Because of a ruling by the Maryland Department of Natural Resources to save the puritan tiger beetle, Mr. and Mrs. Richard Bannister of Lusby, MD, were prevented from taking actions to prevent erosion in the rear of their property which could jeopardize their home. They planned to build a retaining wall at the base of a 60-foot cliff in their backyard, and grade the top to a gentler slope. They were told that any action they took should "not entail destroying tiger beetles." While the Bannisters were wrestling with the bureaucracy, a 15-foot section of their property plunged to the beach below.

PURITAN TIGER BEETLES AND OTHER *COLEOPTERA*

Moses spoke unto the children of Israel, and said:

"Yet these may ye eat of every flying creeping thing that goeth upon all four, which have legs above their feet, to leap withal upon the earth;

"Even these of them ye may eat; the locust after his kind, and the bald locust after his kind, and the beetle after his kind, and the grass hopper after his kind."

Leviticus 11:21 - 11:22

As stated, there are 290,000 species of beetles, and all of them are edible. Usually, the larvae of beetles are more popular as food and are consumed -- raw, fried, or roasted -- by Africans, Australians, Frenchmen, and Americans.   ☞

In China, the diving beetle is raised in freshwater ponds for food, and is considered to be a great delicacy. Beetles are greatly relished by African natives, as well, who eat them in the most diverse forms, boiled, roasted, grilled, salted, dried and reduced to a paste.

If the puritan tiger beetle is like his "endangered" brother, the Northeastern beach tiger beetle, they spend 85% of their lives as larvae and only a few months as mature beetles feeding on dead fish.

Valley Elderberry Longhorn Beetle
Desmocerus californicus dimorphus

The Valley elderberry longhorn beetle, is one of about 400 "species" of longhorn beetles in California. The adults may live as long as three months, feeding on one of three types of elderberry bush, throughout their historic range. But what is their range, and how endangered are they really? To answer this question we only need to look at their distribution.

Once considered endemic to the banks of the Sacramento, American, and San Joaquin Rivers, the elderberry beetle has been found in elderberry bushes along the Merced River, Putah Creek, the Stanislaus River, the Feather River, Consumnes River, and the upper Sacramento River. The listing of the Valley elderberry longhorn beetle on the endangered species list as threatened in 1980, had resounding effects on agriculture and public projects in over eight counties throughout Northern California. How can a two-inch long beetle that lives for three months and has viable breeding populations over several thousand square miles, be remotely considered threatened or endangered?

ELDERBERRY WINE

With the habitat of the Valley elderberry longhorn beetle so plentiful in Europe, North Africa, western Asia, North America, and the West Indies, it seemed appropriate to include a recipe for the elderberry itself. Elderberries are used for making jellies and jams, but they are best known as the basic ingredient for the most famous of homemade wines -- a spicy brew as potent as the maker cares to make it.

12 quarts boiling water	8 whole cloves
4 quarts stemmed elderberries	1 lb. seeded raisins
6-$\frac{3}{4}$ cups sugar	Brandy (optional)
3 t ground ginger	Active dry yeast

Pour boiling water on berries and let stand for 24 hours. Strain through coarse bag or cloth, squeezing and breaking berries to extract all possible juices. Add sugar, ginger, cloves and raisins. Bring to a boil and simmer for 1 hour, skimming frequently. Cool to lukewarm. Add 1/2 cup brandy to each 4 quarts of mixture. Add 1 package of active dry yeast to each 16 quarts of mixture. Let stand for 2 weeks to ferment. Then put in bottles and keep several months in a cool place before using. Makes about 8 quarts.

In Butte County, all protection of portions of the banks of the Sacramento River has been halted in the name of protecting the Valley elderberry longhorn beetle. Without protection of the river banks, the preservation of flood control levees is undermined, threatening flooding of agricultural land as well as entire cities along the river.

In El Dorado County, some 5,500 acres of land was devalued and lost to grazing to protect the beetle. Of this land, 5,300 acres is privately owned.

In an area of Sacramento County, farmers have been required to maintain a 200-yard buffer between farmland and creeks in order to protect the beetle, without compensation for the idled land.

The common threat to all communities where Valley elderberry longhorn beetles reside is the integrity of the levees, where rodents and ground squirrels cannot be controlled. Pesticides and rodenticides are prohibited in or near beetle habitat, allowing burrowing pests to compromise the strength of the levees. Furthermore, land restrictions around the habitat of a "subspecies in abundance that ranges throughout the Central Valley", has had a chilling effect on farming and ranching all over Northern California.

In the winter storms of 1995, two levees of the Pajaro River near Watsonville, California, had breaches causing flooding along a 13 mile stretch of agricultural land. The breaches were caused by the accumulation of trees and debris collected by vegetation along the levees that were protected as species habitat. Agricultural damage was estimated at over $46 million. Is it any wonder that farmers are concerned about the integrity of levees that cannot be preserved because the elderberry bush might be damaged?

TOASTED ELDERBERRY LONGHORN
BEETLE

Beetles are a boon to food gatherers living in arid regions where game is scarce. During the mid-1800's Maj. Howard Egan, a Mormon pioneer, described an Indian "cricket" hunt held near Deep Creek in northern Nevada.

He encountered a group of Indians who, for several days, had been digging five or six trenches, about a foot wide and a foot deep and thirty to forty feet long, joined together at the ends and facing uphill. The Indians covered the trenches with a layer of stiff, dry grass on which the beetles were feeding. During the hottest time of the day, the Indians split up into two groups, with men, women, and children in each, with each person holding a bunch of grass in each hand. Spreading out behind the beetles along the length of the trench, they slowly herded the beetles toward the trenches. When all of the insects had reached the grass covering the trenches, the Indians set fire to the grass held in their hands, and scattered it over the grass on the trenches, creating a big blaze and much smoke, through which the beetles could not crawl out. The women removed the toasted beetles from the trenches, which were now half full of them, and transported them in large baskets back to their camp three or four miles away. Unable to carry off all the beetles in one trip, they returned several times until the trenches were empty.

Barbate June Beetle
Polyphylla barbata

Another beetle that is trying to share full federal protection, although not by its own choosing, is the barbate june beetle. In its larval stage this beetle lives underground, feeding on plant roots. If it is formally declared as endangered, then any kind of digging (whether it be for road maintenance, repairing a septic tank, building a home or anything else) would be a violation. The petition to FWS to add this beetle to the endangered species list argues that it is limited to a few square miles, and business operations in the area may threaten the beetle.

However, further efforts by experts on this beetle, found that its range is about 20 square miles, almost 10 times what the petition stated, and that populations have not changed over the last 45 years. Had this conclusive scientific data not been introduced, the FWS would have listed the beetle as endangered because of "the best available data" listed in the original petition. An excellent example of how data can be manipulated to advance a personal agenda, and lay the burden of proof on others, that a species is not endangered.

BAKED MEALIES AND TOMATOES
Old African Recipe

1 T soft butter, plus 3 T butter cut into $\frac{1}{4}$-inch bits	1 egg, beaten
2 cups fresh beetle larvae	1 t light brown sugar
3 med tomatoes, peeled, seeded and chopped	$1\frac{1}{2}$ t salt
	Ground pepper
	1 cup finely chopped bread crumbs

Preheat oven to 325° F. With a pastry brush, spread the softened butter evenly over the bottom and sides of a $1\frac{1}{2}$-quart baking dish.

In a large bowl, combine the mealies, tomatoes, egg, sugar, salt, and ground pepper, and toss together gently but thoroughly. Pour the mealie mixture into the buttered dish and press it down with a spatula until it is smooth and compact. Sprinkle the top with the bread crumbs and then the 3 tablespoons of butter bits.   ☞

> Bake in the middle of the oven for 1 hour, or until bread crumbs are a rich golden brown. Serve hot, as a vegetable course or a main course at lunch. Serves 4 to 6.
>
> Suggested wine: Van der Hum Liqueur (sweet South African brandy flavored with the peel of the *naartje*, a small tangerine.

Some possible substitutions (except for wine): **American burying beetle, Coffin Cave mold beetle, Delta green ground beetle, Hungerford's crawling water beetle, Kretschmarr Cave mold beetle, Northeastern beach tiger beetle, Tooth Cave ground beetle.**

Bald Eagle
Haliaeetus leucocephalus

Although Benjamin Franklin lobbied extensively for the wild turkey, the United States of America chose the Bald Eagle as our national emblem. And a majestic species it is, deserving of the protection afforded it by law. It feeds on fish primarily, but is also a carrion eater and feasts on dead animals wherever they can be found. They have always been prevalent in Alaska and Canada, but their numbers diminished in the lower forty-eight states to 417 adult pairs in 1963. Today there are over 4,000 nesting pairs in the lower forty-eight states and an additional 45,000 Bald Eagles in Alaska. A success story of the Endangered Species Act? No. The population of the bald eagle was on the rise before the ESA was even adopted, and the population had almost doubled by the time it was listed as endangered. Before a recovery plan had even been drafted, the bald eagle population had almost tripled from its low point. The Bald Eagle Protection Plan of 1940, which prevented shooting of the eagle, and the ban of DDT in 1972, were the sources of this success.

However, even with the resurgence of the bald eagle, and its ultimate declassification from endangered to threatened, the strong arm of the ESA taught Dayton Hyde a hard lesson. Mr. Hyde, an Oregon rancher and noted conservationist, converted 25 percent of his land into wetlands because he loved wildlife and wanted to provide wildlife habitat. At considerable expense, he constructed earthen dams on a stream crossing his land. His newly converted wetland quickly became an attractive wildlife habitat -- a private bird sanctuary, resulting in a substantial increase in the number of bird species on his property. Unfortunately, Mr. Hyde's wetland eventually attracted a population of threatened bald eagles., leading the Government to severely restrict the activity he could conduct on his property. Regulations severely restrict agricultural operations for a 1,500 foot radius around each nest tree, halting any timber harvest, cultivation, mowing or other normal mechanized agricultural operations. Mr. Hyde reports, "My lands have been zoned. I am being regulated for wetlands that weren't there before I created them. Like most of my neighbors, I can save myself from financial disaster only by some creative land management, but the Government has cut out most of my options."

Ironically, Mr. Hyde had founded Operation Stronghold -- a private conservation organization for ranchers and farmers. Membership and certification of this organization required that landowners complete significant programs to protect wildlife and create and maintain habitat. The penalty Mr. Hyde paid for his private stewardship efforts did not go unnoticed by other landowners, however, and Operation Stronghold became a private conservation plan that could not work under the present incentive structure of the ESA.

HYDE'S WILD EAGLE WITH SAUERKRAUT

Bald eagle should be dressed by wet picking. Dip the eagle up and down in hot water heated to 160° F until the coarse wing and tail feathers can be pulled out with ease. Then the bird is wrapped in several folds of muslin and allowed to steam a few minutes. The feathers can then be removed by beginning at the tail end and grasping a handful of feathers, then pushing the feathers out and away from you. After feathers are removed, singe the bird by passing it through a blue flame to remove the pin-feathers and down. Then complete the removal of pin-feathers with tweezers and a sharp knife.

When the feathers and down are completely removed, the eagle should have a baking soda scrub. Rub the baking soda well into the skin, and with a damp cloth, scrub the skin gently but firmly. Rinse well in clear water inside and out, then drain, dry and chill for at least 2 days.

1 dressed eagle	1 quart sauerkraut
2 teaspoons salt	2 apples, diced
$\frac{1}{4}$ cup butter	$\frac{1}{2}$ cup celery
$\frac{3}{4}$ cup chopped onions	$\frac{3}{4}$ t caraway seed

Rub 1 tablespoon baking soda into skin and rinse well inside and out with warm water. Drain. Sprinkle inside and out with the salt. Heat butter, add onions and sauté until lightly browned. Drain the sauerkraut, reserve the liquid. Add the sauerkraut and remaining ingredients to onions. Mix well. Fill cavity of eagle and truss. Place any remaining stuffing in roasting pan around the bird. Bury giblets in this dressing. Cover and bake in a moderate oven (350° F) for 3 hours. Uncover last hour of cooking to brown the eagle. Use the sauerkraut liquid to baste the eagle during the roasting. Make gravy from the sauerkraut juice and drippings as desired. Makes 4 servings.

Suggested Wine: Zinfandel

Another interesting, but unfortunately true, story is about an artist in southern Illinois who makes Indian headdresses. It seems she used feathers she found on the ground, including an eagle feather she picked up at a zoo.

One of the headdresses was used as a gift to Hillary Clinton. Federal wildlife officials heard about it, and Hillary's gift was confiscated. The woman who made the headdress was hauled into federal court, and convicted of violating the laws against possession of protected bird parts. If you pick up a feather in a zoo, or even in your own back yard, you can end up as a convicted felon! Interestingly, President Clinton, shortly thereafter, signed a bill allowing Native Americans to use feathers of endangered birds in religious activities.

Alan and Bonny Riggs of Kingston, WA bought five acres of land on a hillside with a fine view of Puget Sound. They were thrilled to learn that a pair of bald eagles was nesting in a tree 50 feet beyond their property line. Thrilled, that is, until state wildlife officials told them the eagle nest would limit what they could do on their $83,400 parcel.

To get a building permit to build a house, the Riggses had to sign a 32-page eagle management plan calling for nearly all of their newly cleared parcel to revert to forest. They also had to plant a screen of evergreen trees 15 feet in front of their house. That was supposed to block the eagles' view of the house, but it also blocked the house's view of the water.

These regulations were bad enough, but the real kicker came when the wildlife officials deemed the screen of trees was insufficient, and the Riggses were cited criminally and ordered to court.

"It was embarrassing, debilitating, and emotionally draining," Alan Riggs said. "We like the eagles," Bonny Riggs added. "We just wanted to build a house. They have confiscated 90 percent of our property by restriction."

Some possible substitutions: Aleutian Canada goose, American peregrine falcon, Arctic peregrine falcon, Brown pelican, California condor, Hawaiian duck, Hawaiian goose, Hawaiian hawk, Laysan duck, Mariana mallard, Northern Aplomado falcon, Swainson's hawk.

Florida Panther
Felis concolor coryi

The Florida Panther, one of eight cougar subspecies in North America, was believed to be extinct over thirty years ago. It wasn't until 1973 that it was learned that there were survivors in southern Florida. Today, there are still only 50 known Florida panthers confined to 5,000 square miles in Everglades National Park, Big Cypress National Preserve, and the Florida Panther National Wildlife Refuge. Scientists question that an adequate gene pool even exists to maintain a viable population, since this subspecies has already hybridized with Central and South American cougars introduced generations ago. Interstate 75 cuts across the heart of the panther habitat, and numerous overpasses have been constructed at the "natural" crossings of the panther due to many kills by automobile and trucks.

Currently there is a proposal before FWS for a Panther Protection Plan which would include an additional one-million acres of private property. This plan proposes that nearly 500,000 acres of private land be purchased, however an additional 450,000 acres of private land would be regulated to provide habitat. Regulations would lock this property into limited agricultural usage even though it is one of the top ten growth areas in the United States, and studies show that panther populations utilize private property, including citrus groves, without undue regulations.

Since the DNA of the eight North American subspecies of cougar are so similar, scientists have pondered the introduction of western species into Florida, as well as captive breeding, in order to help increase the dwindling populations. Animal rights activists have balked at the plan, however, claiming that it will hybridize a "pure" subspecies. So rather than work to save the species from extinction, extremists are pressuring the Government to lock up more private lands in the name of saving species that obviously don't have a chance without intervention. Where is the logic?

PANTHER CUTLET FORESTER STYLE

2 Lb. of panther cutlets	$\frac{1}{2}$ Lb. of salt pork
1$\frac{1}{2}$ cups of breadcrumbs	2 eggs
1 cup milk	1 T powdered dill
Salt and ground pepper	2 lemons

Cut two pounds of panther steaks about $\frac{1}{2}$ inch thick and pound lightly on a hard surface with a wooden mallet until about $\frac{1}{4}$ inch thick. Sprinkle both sides of the cutlets with powdered dill, rubbing it into the meat, then salt and pepper each cutlet, also rubbing it in. Beat two eggs and one cup of milk and pour into a flat pan. Into another flat pan spread breadcrumbs. Dip the cutlets into the egg mixture and then into the breadcrumbs until both sides are breaded. Put to one side on waxed paper.

Into a large skillet place salt pork, or bacon, sliced thin. Render the fat from the salt pork, then remove the crisp pork. Fry the cutlets in the hot pork fat, then place on brown paper to drain. Serve with a lemon slice. (the crisp salt pork slices can be crumbled into tiny bits and added to a green salad.) Serves 4.

Suggested wine: Petite Sirah

If in fact logic does prevail, and US Fish and Wildlife Service and the Florida Game Commission are able to introduce wild cougars from the West into the Florida panther populations, there are many people from Colorado west to California that would laud that effort.

Although there were no recorded mountain lion attacks on humans in California between 1910 and 1986, there have been numerous accounts of attacks on people since then, and they are on the increase. The state's cougar population is now estimated at 4,000 to 6,000 and the California Fish and Game Department received reports of 350 encounters between cougars and humans in 1994 alone. Up 20% from a year earlier.

In March, 1995 27-year-old Scott Fike was riding his bicycle in the San Gabriel Mountains in southern California when he was attacked. He fought off the animal with rocks and escaped with minor injuries. In December, 1994 56-year-old Iris Kenna was killed while walking alone on a one-lane paved road in Cuyamaca Rancho State Park in San Diego County. She was killed by a 116-pound male lion. In August of 1994, two couples staying at a remote Mendocino County cabin reported killing a mountain lion after it charged them. The confrontation was triggered by a fight between the cougar and their dog. They stabbed the lion to death, and during the struggle one of the men lost his thumb. Tests later indicated the lion had rabies.

MOUNTAIN LION MEATLOAF

$1\frac{1}{2}$ Lb. mountain lion, ground	3 T corn oil
1 egg, lightly beaten	$\frac{1}{4}$ cup cooked rice
$\frac{1}{4}$ cup diced mushrooms	1 T lemon juice
1 chopped green onion	$\frac{1}{4}$ t cayenne pepper
1 cup warm Dark Game Stock	

Preheat oven to 375° F.
Combine all ingredients except stock and knead together well. Place the mixture in a lightly oiled loaf pan and shape into a loaf. Bake 20 minutes. Cover with Dark Game Stock and return to oven. Bake, basting frequently, for an additional 25 minutes. Serve with a cherry sauce. Serves 4.

Suggested wine: Merlot

July, 1994 found a lion in Northern California stalking a house and its inhabitants. On one occasion, the mountain lion ran toward the 3-1/2 year-old daughter of the homeowner, backing off only after shots were fired at it. On another occasion at the same house, mace was used to cause the cougar to retreat, and it was not uncommon for the lion to come up to the porch of the house and walk around. After the mountain lion was killed by Fish and Game, it was determined that the cougar had been feeding on turkeys and goats from ranches in the area. An interesting side of this story is that the lady who asked the authorities to kill the lion asked reporters to not use her name for fear of retaliation from animal rights activists.

Three months before this incident, in April, 1994 Barbara Schoener, 40, was killed by a mountain lion as she was jogging alone in Auburn State Recreation Area northeast of Sacramento, near her home. There was also a fatality in Colorado in January, 1991, when an 18 year-old jogger was killed as he ran alone on a trail less than half a mile from his high school in Idaho Springs. And 51 year-old Lucy Gomez was found dead in the Sierra foothills of Butte County, having been killed by a mountain lion in November, 1988.

SWEET AND SOUR PANTHER ROAST

3 to 5 Lb. panther roast	1 cup wine vinegar
3 tablespoons fat	$\frac{3}{4}$ cup brown sugar
2 sliced onions	$\frac{1}{2}$ t nutmeg

Cook onions in vinegar in Dutch oven or large kettle until transparent. Remove onions and save. Brown panther roast well on both sides. Add onions, vinegar, brown sugar and nutmeg. Stir liquid around roast until well mixed. Cover tightly. Simmer about 3 or $3\frac{1}{2}$ hours until meat is tender. If liquid is not thick enough when meat is removed, thicken with cornstarch for a flavorful gravy. Serves 6 to 8.

Suggested wine: Cabernet Sauvignon

Ten year old Lisa Kowalski was attacked and bitten on the buttocks at Cuyamaca Rancho State Park while she played ball with her father in September, 1993. Devon Foote, 6, was attacked in Los Padres National Forest in Santa Barbara in August 1993. In March, 1992 Darron Arroyo, 9, suffered minor injuries in a cougar attack in Gaviota State Park, also in Santa Barbara County. Justin Mellon, 6, received minor injuries in an attack in Orange County's Caspers Regional Park. Laura Small, 4, was not quite so lucky. She was attacked in Caspers Regional Park seven months earlier and left partially paralyzed and blind in one eye.

Management of *Felis concolor*, (also known as mountain lion, cougar, panther, or puma) in western states, by means of sport hunting as well as trapping and relocating, could bring the populations in line and prevent further damage or injury. With proper management, rather than the typical hands off approach so often implemented, we could have viable populations of panthers in Florida, California, and anywhere else deemed worthy.

Some possible substitutions: Eastern cougar, Jaguarundi, Margay, Ocelot, Puma.

Mount Graham Red Squirrel
Tamiasciurus hudsonicus grahamensis

An observatory construction project in Graham County, Arizona was halted when a conflict arose around the Mt. Graham red squirrel. The observatory project, to be located in the Pinaleno Mountains on Forest Service property, was managed by the University of Arizona with backing by the Smithsonian, the Vatican, and the Italian and German governments.

In their jeopardy consultation, where they are to suggest "reasonable and prudent alternatives" to development in order to protect endangered species, the US Fish and Wildlife Service made every effort to have the project dropped. FWS biologist Lesley Fitzpatrick admitted that the Regional Office suggested features that would make the development unpalatable to the Forest Service and the University. She stated, "FWS did not want to take a stand against development but hoped to make their suggestion a poison pill that would cause the Forest Service to reject development or the University to abandon the project...(the suggestion) was a 'laundry list' and it referred to every feature we could include, in addition to the ones needed by the red squirrel, that would make the project unattractive to the proponent or unpopular internally to the Forest Service."

MT. GRAHAM RED SQUIRREL BRUNSWICK STEW

Brunswick County, North Carolina, Brunswick County, Virginia, and Brunswick, Georgia all claim credit for the origination of this stew. Therefore, feel free to substitute the Carolina northern flying squirrel (*Glaucomys sabrinus coloratus*), the Virginia northern flying squirrel (*G. s. fuscus*) or other listed substitutions, in this recipe.

2 red squirrels	2 cups strained
1 tablespoon salt	tomatoes
4 potatoes, peeled and cubed	$\frac{1}{4}$ lb. diced salt
1 cup canned corn	pork
2 diced onions	1T butter
1 cup lima beans	1 T flour
$\frac{1}{2}$ t ground pepper	$\frac{1}{2}$ cup sherry

Skin, dress, draw, and clean squirrels. Disjoint. Put 8 cups water and salt in kettle. Bring to boil. Add squirrels, potatoes, corn, onions, beans, tomatoes, sherry, and salt pork. Cover and simmer $2\frac{1}{2}$ hours, stirring every 30 minutes. Add flour, mixed to a smooth paste with butter. Mix well. Cover and cook 15 minutes more. Season with pepper and stir until slightly thickened. Serves 6.

Suggested Wine: Cabernet Sauvignon

The observatory project proceeded, and the Mt. Graham red squirrel, a subspecies of the abundant, common red squirrel, is flourishing. And this despite the fact that the FWS have stated in their recovery plan that it will take at least 300 years to restore the Mount Graham Red Squirrel habitat.

Some possible substitutions: Carolina Northern flying squirrel, Delmarva Peninsula fox squirrel, Nelson's antelope ground squirrel, Virginia Northern flying squirrel.

Conservancy Fairy Shrimp
Longhorn Fairy Shrimp
Vernal Pool Fairy Shrimp
Streptocephalus

Detected for the first time by humans in 1990, these tiny crustaceans find home in irrigation ditches, ponds, truck ruts, and just about any place that a small body of water collects even for a short period. Biological cousin's of the "sea monkeys" that used to be sold in ads in the back of comic books and shipped by mail across the country, the fairy shrimp are just as hearty and by most accounts can be found by the millions. They are found in the Central Valley region of California, as well as Europe, Asia, Australia and Africa.

The surprising thing about the listing of the fairy shrimp, was the speed in which they were listed. Six months after their discovery, Roxanne Bittman, a botanist, petitioned the US Fish and Wildlife Service to list them as endangered. The agency formally proposed the listing in 1992, and final listing came in September of 1994. In listing the fairy shrimp, the FWS does not claim they are in danger of extinction, but that their habitat -- mud holes -- are "imperiled".

CONSERVANCY FAIRY SHRIMP
CANAPÉS

3 tablespoons butter	$\frac{2}{3}$ cup rich milk
3 tablespoons flour	$\frac{1}{3}$ cup white wine
$\frac{1}{2}$ t curry powder	1 t Worcestershire
$\frac{1}{4}$ t salt	$\frac{1}{2}$ lb. cooked shrimp

Melt butter; add flour, curry powder and salt. Stir in milk, wine, and Worcestershire sauce. Cook and stir over low heat until mixture is thickened. Add Fairy shrimp, stirring lightly. Serve warm on toast rounds or crisp crackers.

Suggested Wine: Sherry

Developers opposed to the listing hired their own environmental consultants who did an extensive study and found 1,226 vernal pools containing fairy shrimp -- probably only a small fraction of the total number. And far from becoming extinct, vernal pools cover roughly one million acres in California, not to mention irrigation ditches, tire ruts, and other mud holes this 5/8" little shrimp calls home.

Although FWS bureaucrats went ahead with the listing, saying that it would only affect a "small fraction, if that" of development in the Central Valley, it already has had its effect. A pony ranch that housed a program for needy and disabled children has been shut down, mining operations have been halted, undetermined costs to farming and ranching that will continue to mount, and an estimated $500 million cost to the housing industry over the next ten years.

LONGHORN FAIRY SHRIMP
IN TOMATO ASPIC

1 envelope unflavored gelatin	10 stuffed olives
$1\frac{3}{4}$ cups V-8 juice	1 T lemon juice
2 T Chili Pepper Catsup	$\frac{1}{8}$ t lemon pepper and garlic salt
2 cup Longhorn F. shrimp	1 cup diced celery

Add lemon juice to shrimp. Sprinkle gelatin on $\frac{1}{2}$ cup cold V-8 juice. Heat remainder of V-8 with catsup, pepper and garlic salt. Add softened gelatin, stir until thoroughly dissolved. Cool until unbeaten egg white consistency. Add shrimp, celery and sliced stuffed olives. Pour into ring mold and chill until firm. Turn out on cake plate. Fill center with canned green asparagus spears and garnish with sliced hard boiled eggs plus your favorite salad dressing. Serve with toasted bread sticks.

Suggested Wine: Dubonet

VERNAL POOL FAIRY SHRIMP COCKTAIL SAUCE

$\frac{3}{4}$ cup chili sauce
2 T horseradish
$\frac{1}{2}$ t grated onion

3 T lemon juice
2 t Worcestershire
    sauce

Combine all ingredients; mix well; add salt, pepper, and hot sauce to taste. Chill. Serve with Fairy Shrimp Cocktail. Makes $1\frac{1}{4}$ cups sauce. Serve shrimp with toothpicks and tweezers.

Some possible substitutions: Alabama cave shrimp, California freshwater shrimp, Cave crayfish, Chimney cave shrimp, Kentucky cave shrimp, Nashville crayfish, Shasta crayfish.

Wyoming Toad
Bufo hemiophrys baxteri

The Wyoming toad, considered a relic of the glacial era, whose only chances of restoration across its previous range is another ice age, was probably doomed with extinction before man knew of its existence. However, US Fish and Wildlife continues to spend hundred's of thousands of dollars annually for its protection.

The newest proposal to protect the toad calls for the banning of 43 pesticides over 970 square miles, even though only four square miles of it is toad habitat, near Albany County, Wyoming.

FRENCH-FRIED WYOMING TOAD LEGS

2 lb. toad legs	2 Tablespoons water
2 teaspoons salt	1 cup fine bread
$\frac{1}{4}$ teaspoon pepper	crumbs
2 eggs, beaten	Fat for frying
4 teaspoons lemon juice	

If toad legs are large, cut apart through backbone. Never wash as the delicate flavor is easily lost. If necessary, cut off feet and wipe with a damp cloth. Dry on paper towel. Season with salt and pepper. Combine egg, lemon juice and water. Dip toad legs into egg mixture and then roll in bread crumbs. Fry in deep fat at 350° F for 6 to 10 minutes or golden brown and until tender. Serve immediately. 4 to 5 servings.

Suggested Beverage: Red Tail Ale

The ban would stymie farming, ranching, gardening, tourism and recreation in the area, as well as efforts to protect thousands of people from mosquitoes. Wyoming state officials say there is no scientific evidence that pesticides are even threatening the Wyoming toad. In fact the main factor affecting the recovery of the Wyoming toad, a subspecies of the Manitoba toad, has been a bacterial disease known as red leg.

Some possible substitutions: Houston toad, Puerto Rico crested toad, Pine Barrens treefrog.

Red-cockaded Woodpecker
Picoides borealis

The red-cockaded woodpecker, fondly known as the "spotted owl of the south", makes its home in the abundant pine forests in the southeastern part of the country. It has become the surrogate species of preservationists to halt all timber harvesting of the various pine species that are over 60 years old -- hardly considered "old growth". The problem is, almost 80 percent of the marketable Southern pine is found on private property from Texas to North Carolina, and from Delaware to Florida. As pines get older, many suffer from a fungus called "heart rot", and the normally hard heart wood of the tree becomes soft, dry, and easily excavated by the woodpecker. Although certainly not limited to nesting in 60 year old pines, the red-cockaded woodpecker prefers the path of least resistance.

This partiality for older pines has created a dichotomy for land owners who, as true conservationists, want to manage their timber land for the sustainability of their timber, yet are often punished for creating habitat for the woodpeckers. This is exactly what happened to Benjamin Cone, Jr.

Cone, who owns 8,000 acres of timber outside of Greensboro, North Carolina, had been harvesting his timber on a sustainable yield basis allowing some of his trees to mature to 60-80 years old. He wanted to create some good bird habitat on his property, and by clearing underbrush, and practicing sound forestry, Mr. Cone had created prime nesting for the red-cockaded woodpecker. Now 1,600 acres of his land is called home by the woodpecker, and the Endangered Species Act forbids him to cut any of the timber or do anything else to endanger the bird's habitat.

Mr. Cone spent over $8,000 for biologists to make sure he follows the stringent rules, and estimates it has cost another $1.8 million in lost revenues. Not being able to afford the rest of his property to become woodpecker habitat, Mr. Cone will have to accelerate his harvesting and change his forest management practices. "I cannot afford to let those woodpeckers take over the rest of my property. I'm going to start massive clear-cutting. I'm going to a 40-year rotation instead of a 70 to 80-year rotation." As R.J. Smith, of the Competitive Enterprise Institute in Washington, DC said, "The perverse incentive of the ESA accelerates destruction of the very habitat the act was designed to protect."

ROAST RED-COCKADED WOODPECKER
WITH CHIVES DRESSING

4 dressed woodpeckers	$\frac{3}{4}$ teaspoon salt
Giblets, finely chopped	ground pepper
$\frac{1}{3}$ cup finely chopped celery	1 egg, beaten
2 Tablespoons butter	3 T chopped chives
$\frac{1}{2}$ lb. rye bread crumbs	12 slices bacon
$\frac{3}{4}$ cup water	1 Tablespoon flour
$\frac{2}{3}$ cup milk	$\frac{1}{4}$ cup white wine

Remove pin feathers and singe woodpeckers. Rinse well inside and out with warm water. Drain thoroughly. Tear bread into small crumbs (there should be 1 quart of crumbs packed loosely). Sauté celery and giblets in butter for 5 minutes. Remove from heat, add water, cool and pour over crumbs. Add seasoning, egg and chives; toss lightly to mix.

☞

Pack into salted cavity of woodpeckers and truss. Lay bacon slices over breasts and tops of legs and place, breast up, on rack in roaster. Cover and bake in a moderately slow oven (325° F) for about 2 hours. Remove cover and roast $\frac{1}{2}$ hour longer to brown woodpeckers. Turn off heat, place woodpeckers in the cover of roaster, cover with foil and set back into oven to keep hot. (Neat trick using the cover.) Skim off all but 2 Tablespoons of fat. Prepare gravy from drippings, flour, milk and wine.

Suggested wine: Chianti

In an ironic twist, the same type of habitat that is being protected in the Pacific Northwest is being destroyed in east Texas for the sake of this endangered bird. The woodpecker does not like hardwood trees that grow in the pines, so conservationists are destroying hardwood seedlings that might impede the woodpecker species. In Louisiana, small, family-owned tree farms are being managed in a defensive manner due to strict ESA enforcement. Tree farmers are selling their larger trees as a defensive measure to ensure the red-cockaded woodpecker does not establish itself on their property. The act itself encourages property owners to take whatever means necessary to keep endangered species off their land.

Henry Bynum, who owns 1,600 acres of land in Williamsburg County in South Carolina, is worried about his property. The land had been in his family for over 40 years, passed down from the previous generation, and held as a sort of savings account. Although his family does not depend on timber harvest income, he hoped to someday pass it on to his children, to be cut and reforested as it had in the past. "It looks like I'll be passing it to the woodpeckers," Bynum laments.

RED-COCKADED WOODPECKER
SOUR CREAM FRICASSEE

4 to 6 woodpeckers	$\frac{1}{4}$ cup shortening
$\frac{1}{2}$ cup flour	1 large onion
1 Tablespoon paprika	2 cups hot water
1 Tablespoon salt	1 cup sour cream

Dress, singe, clean and wash red-cockaded woodpeckers. Cut in serving portions and dredge in the flour mixed with paprika and salt. Brown slowly on all sides in shortening. Add sliced onion during last stage of browning bird and cook until soft. Add any flour mixture left from the dredging, blend well with drippings, then add water all at once. Stir to blend flour with liquid, then cover and simmer $1\frac{1}{2}$ hours or until woodpecker is tender. Add sour cream and simmer 5 minutes.

Suggested Wine: Grey Riesling

Dwight Stewart, a private forester, along with two partners, have also been plagued with the red-cockaded woodpecker, but not because they nested in any of their trees. Their 10,000 acres of land was under restrictions because woodpeckers on neighboring US Forest Service property foraged there. The Forest Service finally ended up buying the property, but thousands of dollars were lost on the timber they could not harvest. Stewart states plainly, "There's going to have to be some compromises. If we don't, people are not going to manage for the red-cockaded woodpecker." (Or for any other species, for that matter.)

Webb Smathers, a wildlife economist at Clemson University, proposes giving landowners economic credits for having birds reproduce on their property. The more juvenile birds produced, the more credits earned. Young birds eventually could be moved to a public forest set up as a recovery site, and the privately owned timber could be harvested. This is similar to the pact between Westvaco and the US Fish and Wildlife Service discussed earlier in this book. It could be expanded upon, to the benefit of all, as it was with an agreement between the Government and Georgia-Pacific in 1993.

Under the pact signed in April, 1993, Georgia-Pacific will take special precautions around the 112 groups of red-cockaded woodpeckers found on their 4.2 million acres of timberland in Arkansas, Mississippi, Louisiana, South Carolina, and North Carolina. However, by signing this agreement, and subsequently sacrificing a portion of the profits of their timber holdings, the Government will allow them to manage the rest of their forest land. Interior Secretary, Bruce Babbitt says of this agreement, "It's a demonstration that it is possible on a large cooperative scale to find that balance between the imperative to create jobs in forest production and the imperative to protect the environment." However, until that imperative is included in all species listings on a nationwide and permanent basis, try:

RED-COCKADED WOODPECKER SPAGHETTI

3 large stalks celery, diced	3 pinches rosemary
1 large onion, diced	3 cups diced
2 cloves garlic, minced	woodpecker
1-2 pinches marjoram	5 small cans tomato
1-2 pinches oregano	paste
8 Tablespoons butter	2 med cans tomatoes

Sauté in butter until tender, the onions and celery, then add red-cockaded woodpecker and brown. Add herbs and stir to mix well. Then add tomatoes and tomato paste. Let simmer all day, adding water when necessary. Serve over spaghetti noodles. Left over sauce freezes well.

Suggested Wine: Hearty Burgundy

It seems that the red-cockaded woodpecker hasn't just infected privately owned and publicly owned commercial timber land, either. The small seven inch bird thrives in the piney woods of Fort Bragg, North Carolina. When environmental groups threatened to sue in 1990 under the Endangered Species Act, the Army restricted its training for some of its most elite units, including the 82nd Airborne Division. Instead of being able to freely travel through the training area in the woods, troops must steer clear of 430 woodpecker habitats scattered across the 150,000-acre fort.

"Fort Bragg has attempted to comply with the law to protect these species -- but at the expense of training readiness for the units that will be first in battle," said retired Gen. Carl Steiner. Maj. Gen. Richard Davis, Steiner's successor at Fort Bragg, said the woodpecker protection policy has created some "bad habits." In war games for example, "commanders can turn to the map of woodpecker sites for clues into where opposing forces might go," he said.

Since 1990, the Army has spent $6.8 million to comply with the Endangered Species Act, most of it relating to efforts to protect the woodpeckers from rolling tanks and flying bullets, which they had managed to survive from for 70 years.

The law allows the defense secretary to override the species protection practices if he believes they harm national security. However, the environmental lobby, and the threat of lawsuits by preservationists, has become so powerful, three successive defense secretaries have refused to do so.

Some possible substitutions: Hawaiian crow, Hawaiian dark-rumped petrel, Ivory billed woodpecker, Marbled murrelet, Mariana crow, Maui parrotbill, Puerto Rico parrot, Puerto Rico plain pigeon, White-necked crow, Wood stork.

Delhi Sands Flower-Loving Fly
Rhaphiomidas terminatus abdominalis

The Endangered Species Act had a derisive effect on the construction of the San Bernadino County Medical Center, to the tune of $3,310,199. This was the cost to mitigate for the presence of eight (that's right, eight) Delhi Sands flower-loving flies, one of over 16,000 species of flies. The effort as negotiated with the US Fish and Wildlife Service and the California Department of Fish and Game resulted in moving and redesigning the facility to provide 1.92 acres of protected habitat for eight flies believed to occupy the site. The effort mitigates only for species on site. Cost per fly amounted to $413,774.25 each, of taxpayers money, and resulted in a one-year construction delay. This cost is equivalent to the average cost of treatment of 494 inpatients or 23,644 outpatients. The average life span of the adult Delhi Sands flower-loving fly is one to two weeks.

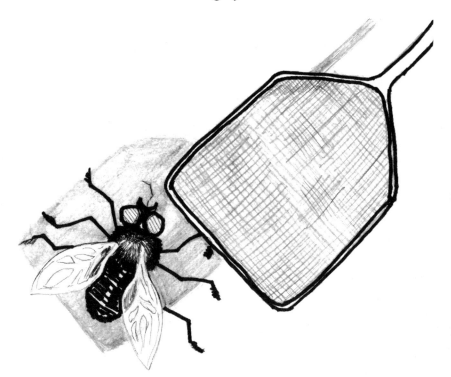

Black-capped Vireo
Vireo atricapillus

In 1985, Beth Morian, a lifelong environmentalist and member of the board of directors of the Zoological Society of Houston, learned that 34 pairs of the Black-capped vireo had been found on and around her family's 1300-acre ranch west of Austin, Texas.

Rather than immediately clear and develop the land, as they could have done legally, Morian donated 62 acres, worth $1.9 million, to the city of Austin for a nature preserve. Then they started to sell 66 home sites on 89 of their remaining acres, investing $2 million to develop the property.

In the meantime, the US Fish and Wildlife Service listed the vireo as endangered, and froze all development and use of over half of their property. Nice reward for trying to provide a nature preserve for the public at large.

BLACK-CAPPED VIREO PURLEAU

Small game birds, such as the black-capped vireo, California gnatcatcher and the Florida scrub jay, need to be handled with care. First, the small birds should be dry plucked and *not* skinned. Also, unless the vireo is to be eaten the same day it is killed, it should be hung in a cooling room where the temperature ranges between 40° and 45°. Another important practice is that these birds should be drawn by making a small cut above the vent and removing the viscera through this opening. The smaller the orifice for drawing, the less chance the bird will dry out in cooking. ☞

8 black-capped vireo	$\frac{1}{2}$ lb. butter
1 cup canned tomatoes	2 small onions
1 t marjoram	1 cup flour
$\frac{1}{2}$ t basil	1 clove garlic
4 cups chicken stock	salt
2 cups white rice	lemon pepper

Place flour, marjoram, salt and pepper in a large paper bag. Split the vireo down the spine and breast. Shake the half-birds in the paper bag until well dusted, then put to one side. Melt $\frac{1}{2}$ lb. butter in a large kettle over a medium flame, add one split clove of garlic and brown it well, then remove garlic and throw away. Brown the birds well but quickly in the butter, then remove them to a warming oven.

Rinse rice with cold water. Prepare 1 cup of chopped, canned tomatoes, without the juice, and dice 2 small onions. Brown the onions in the butter, add tomatoes and stir for two minutes. Add the rice and continue stirring until the rice is slightly browned. Prepare in advance 4 cups of chicken stock with $\frac{1}{2}$ t basil. Place the halved vireos in the kettle, stir them with the rice, then add the four cups of chicken stock. Bring to a boil, stirring constantly, then reduce the heat to a minimum simmer, cover and do not disturb for 25 minutes. Remove from stove, stir the contents carefully, place in a large, deep platter, and serve.

Suggested beverage: Elderberry wine or hard cider

The Black-capped vireo, also on the top ten list of spending for recovery at over $53 million, has declined over the years, because of a predator. Not the human kind that has so often been blamed for the demise of nature, but another bird. The brown-headed cowbird forages in open spaces, and then lays its eggs in other birds' nests. The cowbird chicks, hatching quickly, push their non-cowbird nestmates over the side, thus eliminating the chance for the vireo or other species of birds to mature and multiply. I'm waiting now for the FWS, in all its wisdom, to list the brown-headed cowbird as endangered, since it can't find suitable habitat in which to lay its eggs.

Some possible substitutions: Bridled white-eye, California least tern, Laysan finch, Least bell's vireo, Least tern, Nihoa finch, Piping plover, Roseate tern.

Blunt-nosed Leopard Lizard
Crotaphytus silus

Near Fresno, California, Ted Off and his cousins ran Tule Vista Farms, a dairy ranch. One year, not long ago, they plowed 160 acres of their 315-acre parcel to plant barley for feed. Soon after, an armed US marshal and several FWS agents showed up with a search warrant. They were looking for body parts of the blunt-nosed leopard lizard. After crisscrossing the 160 acre section of the farm in several vehicles for nearly a day, they found no lizards or lizard parts on the farm.

The FWS agents, however, still threatened the Off family with criminal charges, maintaining the Offs had destroyed critical lizard habitat, and filed suit against them. To avoid an expensive legal battle, an out-of-court settlement was reached. They agreed to pay a $5,000 fine, give 60 acres of their land to the Federal Government, plead guilty to destroying habitat, sell the remaining 100 acres to FWS through the Nature Conservancy, and to "donate" $14,000 for long term management of the parcel. The land is now part of the Pixley National Wildlife Refuge.

BLUNT-NOSED LEOPARD LIZARD
MATELOTE

2-3 Blunt-nosed leopard lizards, skinned	1 t fresh thyme
	1 bay leaf
8 sprigs fresh parsley	1 onion, sliced
4 shallots, sliced	2 cloves garlic
Salt and pepper to taste	2 stalks celery
1 bottle Burgundy wine	$\frac{1}{2}$ cup cognac
16 pearl onions	6 T butter
16 mushroom caps	Juice 1 lemon
1 T each, flour and butter mixed	$\frac{1}{2}$ cup parsley

Rinse skinned and cleaned blunt nosed leopard lizards with head and tail removed in cold water and pat dry. Cut into 2-inch pieces, and place pieces in large baking pan. Add thyme, bay leaf, parsley, sliced onion, sliced shallots, chopped garlic, salt and pepper, and chopped celery. Cover the lizard meat with wine. Place pan on stove and bring to a slow boil. Add cognac and simmer for 5 minutes or until lizard meat is tender. Remove lizard meat from pan.

Boil sauce about 5 minutes to reduce. Strain sauce and reserve.

Sauté pearl onions in butter until brown and tender. Cover the pan and continue cooking onions until they are soft. Add mushroom caps and sauté for a few minutes (mushrooms should remain firm). Add lemon juice to onion-mushroom mixture.

Return wine sauce to the stove. Bring to a quick boil, and add butter-flour mixture to thicken sauce to the consistency of light cream. Remove sauce from heat and pour over the lizard meat; add onions and mushrooms. Sprinkle with fresh chopped parsley. Serve with rice or boiled new potatoes. Serves 4.

Suggested wine: Chokecherry wine (homemade)

The USFWS has used threats and intimidation, fines, and out-right taking of private property, because their own recovery plan for the blunt-nosed leopard lizard says "A current target acreage figure of 80,000 acres has been established for the San Joaquin Valley floor, with additional emphasis on optional habitats containing high density blunt-nosed leopard lizard." They go on to say, "conflicting land users will be reduced or eliminated in an effort to restore habitat to optimal condition." This is the United States Fish and Wildlife Service saying that land users will be "reduced or eliminated" to save habitat? How, might be the question we should all be asking ourselves.

Some possible substitutions: Blue-tailed mole skink, Coachella Valley fringe-toed lizard, Island night lizard, Mona ground iguana, Monito gecko, Sand skink, St. Croix ground lizard.

Desert Tortoise
Gopherus agassizii

A 90-home subdivision in Utah was brought to a standstill when five "endangered" desert tortoises wandered onto the site. The tortoises could not be removed because their habitat is protected by the Endangered Species Act. Listing of the desert tortoise ignores the fact that there are an estimated 2.5 million in existence. This species' biggest threat is not man, but rather a respiratory disease and predatory ravens. Experts agree the raven is the primary cause of decline in the tortoise population. The ravens kill juvenile tortoises thus preventing them from maturing and bearing offspring. Shortly after the tortoise's listing, however, the Humane Society of the United States and other wildlife groups, halted a Bureau of Land Management raven control program on the grounds that the program would adversely affect the raven. The tortoise also has created similar problems in California, Nevada, Arizona and New Mexico, where protection efforts of the species have halted livestock grazing, mining and development.

Federal wildlife regulators designated 6.4 million acres of Southwestern desert as critical habitat for the desert tortoise in February 1994. Included in the area is federally owned property known as Ward Valley, which was designated as a dump site for the biotech, medical and research industries which generate low-level nuclear waste. After spending about $40 million in engineering and environmental studies, the contractor under license by California, has had to halt the project.

Later that same year, just prior to adjourning, Congress passed the California Desert Protection Act. This put aside nearly 8 million acres of desert in a new mega-National Park. The 12,000 square mile area, larger than the State of Maryland, encompasses the existing Joshua Tree National Park and Death Valley National Monument, and the East Mojave National Scenic Area and adds 3 million acres to the park system. This, at a time when the National Park Service, by its own admission, is running a 37-year $5.6 billion backlog in capital construction and maintenance costs, and a 26-year $1.2 billion backlog in land acquisition.

DESERT TORTOISE PREPARATION

In 1945, the US Fish and Wildlife Service described the dressing of a turtle as follows: "The first step in dressing is the removal of the head. They can be made to protrude their heads by applying pressure with the foot to the back or upper part of the shell. After the head is well stretched out, the head can be cut off. Then, run a sharp knife around the edges of the skin where it joins the shell. Pull back the skin over the legs to the feet which are then disjointed. The lower part of the shell or plastron is then removed by cutting through the bridges which join the upper and lower shells, cutting close to the lower part of the shell. ☞

The bridge may be cut with a sharp knife, or if necessary, a hatchet or saw. Having cut the bridges, the plastron may be readily removed by inserting a sharp knife just under it and lifting it off. This done, the entails may be extracted with very little trouble, and the four quarters easily taken out of the upper shell. If one wishes to save the tenderloin in the upper part or 'ceiling' of the upper shell, the ribs may be cut with a hatchet. This may appear to be a lengthy and complicated process, but it is simpler than killing, plucking and drawing a chicken."

From *Cooking Wild Game* by Frank G. Ashbrook and Edna N Sater, 1945, Orange Judd Publishing, New York, NY.

Under this recently passed Desert Protection Act, however, private property owners won a victory of sorts. The Act would have the Government acquire 700,000 acres of private land in the California desert. George Framton, Department of the Interior Assistant Secretary for Fish, Wildlife and Parks, has said that the acquisition costs can be greatly reduced because of the presence of the Desert Tortoise and other ESA listed species. In other words, since ESA listed species are on private property, the Government can restrict the use of that land, thus devaluing it for their own benefit.

However, the Tauzin/Hansen amendment to the Act, provides that lands acquired by the Federal Government under the bill shall be appraised "without regard to the presence of threatened or endangered species." Score one for the property owner.

DESERT TORTOISE SOUP

$1\frac{1}{2}$ qt strained chicken stock 1 medium onion
1 lb. desert tortoise meat 1 T chopped
   (w/o bone or gristle)   parsley
3 T butter 5-6 slices lemon

Prepare Desert tortoise as described above. Prepare a richly flavored chicken stock seasoned only with salt. Strain. Cut tortoise meat into small chunks. Brown slowly in the butter. Add chopped onion and sauté slowly over medium heat until onion is soft and yellow. Add tortoise, onion seasoning and any butter to chicken stock, heat to boiling, reduce heat and simmer gently for 10 minutes. Serve with a sprinkling of parsley on each bowl of soup and a paper-thin slice of lemon floated on top. 5 to 6 servings.

Suggested Wine: Chardonnay

Because the Government settled the lawsuit with the Humane Society to halt raven control, the Feds felt they had to take other action as well. In Nevada, they limited the grazing rights of cattlemen and woolgrowers, canceled off-highway vehicle events, denied permits to mining companies, and shut down the building boom in the fastest growing city in the country, Las Vegas.

The desert tortoise is common in the land surrounding Las Vegas. In order to continue to build downtown, the city of Las Vegas agreed to place 400,000 acres of surrounding Clark County in a Desert Tortoise Management Zone, where there will be no grazing, no mining, no off-road vehicle events, no hunting, and no hiking. In all, Las Vegas surrendered a total of 1.4 million acres of Clark County and nearby Lincoln County to the Desert Tortoise Management Zone, all because the Government did not have the courage to fight the Humane Society.

TORTOISE A LA KING

2 Tablespoons butter	2 cups cooked
1 cup sliced mushrooms	tortoise, diced
2 Tablespoons flour	1 pimento
1 teaspoon salt	ground pepper
2 cups milk	

Melt butter. Add mushrooms. Cover and cook about 5 minutes. Sprinkle with flour. Add all other ingredients. Let cook until sauce thickens. Serve on toast or in patty shells. Serves 8.

Suggested wine: Chenin Blanc

Some possible substitutions: Alabama red-bellied turtle, Flattened musk turtle, Gopher tortoise, Green sea turtle, Hawksbill sea turtle, Kemp's Ridley sea turtle, Leatherback sea turtle, Loggerhead sea turtle, Olive Ridley sea turtle, Plymouth red-bellied turtle, Ringed sawback turtle, Yellow-blotched map turtle.

Gray Bat
Myotis grisescens

Although bats are a special friend of man, primarily eating thousands of insects as it flies with its mouth open, and needs only an undisturbed cave for winter hibernation and summer birthing, I came upon a disconcerting article in *The Wall Street Journal* that bears mentioning here.

Heidi Hughes of the American Bat Conservation Society says that bats "have been horribly maligned for centuries by Anglo-Saxon Western culture." (I wonder if she spit those words out with rancor, "Anglo-Saxon Western culture"). In an attempt to de-fang the public's politically incorrect response to the winged creatures of the night, the Rockville, Maryland society is introducing a line of Halloween treats called Vampire Bat Bites. The cream filled chocolate candies are shaped like "cute and adorable" vampire bats, the society says.

The chocolates are the bat society's latest attempt to create a warm and fuzzy image for bats. "People think of bats as rodents with wings," Ms Hughes says. "We think of them as being little miniature kittens."

But public health officials are outraged. According to the Center for Disease Control and Prevention, bats are the No. 1 cause of rabies in humans in the United States.

"Bat bites kill people," says Mark S. Rapoport, commissioner of health in New York. He calls the candy "macabre" and says "it more than trivializes" the danger of contact with bats. He believes strongly that when it comes to bats, a little fear is a good thing. Trying to make small children warm up to bats is "a terrible idea."

An 11-year-old girl died last year in New York, from a strain of rabies carried by bats. It was the first rabies death in New York in forty years, and has doctors exceedingly worried. They feel the Bat Conservation Society's mission is not only dangerous, but in poor taste as well. (No pun intended.)

POTTED BAT EASTLAKE

Except for the polar regions, high mountaintops, and a few remote islands, bats of one species or another live all around the world in very large numbers. It is estimated one fourth of all mammals on Earth are bats, comprised of some 951 species. Ranging in size from the 0.052-ounce Kitti's hog-nosed bat to the Samoan flying fox, which has a wing span of $6\frac{1}{2}$ feet.

Like most other mammals, bats are eaten in various parts of the world. The large flying foxes, which weigh up to 3 pounds, are highly esteemed as food in Africa and Australia. Bats in general are also popular in parts of China and Asia. Interestingly, a large fruit bat in the Philippines is hunted not only for its meat, but also for its fur. (all bats, being mammals, are covered with fine hair instead of feathers.) With so many bats, and of varied sizes, the gastronomic possibilities are endless. This is just one from the Southwest.

1 to 5 bats, depending on size   bay leaf
salt and ground pepper   chopped onion

Skin, clean and hang bat for a couple of days with wings removed. Cut the bat in quarters when ready to cook. Place bats in large kettle and cover with cold water, add the seasonings and boil until the meat falls off the bones. Remove the bones. Place the bats and the liquid in a bowl and chill overnight in the refrigerator, or until it jellies. Serve cold on bed of lettuce or on bread.

Suggested beverage: Homemade Beer or Fig Wine

Some possible substitutions: Hawaiian hoary bat, Indiana bat, Little Mariana fruit bat, Mariana fruit bat, Mexican long-nosed bat, Ozark big-earred bat, Sanborn's long-nosed bat, Virginia big-earred bat.

Colorado Squawfish
Ptyshocheilus lucius

The Colorado Squawfish, along with the Humpback Chub, Bonytail Chub, and Razorback Sucker, have been considered trash fish for most of the century. They feed on young trout and salmon and are found in Arizona, California, Colorado, New Mexico, Nevada, Utah, Wyoming, and Washington. In fact, up until a few years ago, the US Fish and Wildlife Service was using poison to get rid of the fish. However, that same FWS has now listed them as endangered, and they rank in the top ten recovery plans in respect to dollars spent. Through 1993, over $57 million had been spent on their recovery, and the extended economic impacts are expected to exceed $650 million.

BAKED SQUAWFISH WITH CAPER BUTTER

4 Colorado squawfish fillets
$\frac{1}{3}$ cup fresh lemon juice
$\frac{1}{2}$ cup butter, melted
Salt and ground pepper
$\frac{1}{4}$ cup each chopped parsley
        and capers

Rub the squawfish fillets with lemon juice and brush them well with melted butter. Season with salt and pepper to taste. Arrange in a baking dish and bake in a preheated hot oven (425° F) for about 20 minutes, basting with a combination of melted butter and lemon juice every 5 minutes. Do not turn.

Arrange the cooked squawfish fillets on a hot platter. Mix the pan juices with the chopped parsley and capers, and pour over the fillets. If additional liquid is needed, add a little dry vermouth or white wine. Good with new potatoes, dressed with butter and parsley, and a cucumber salad. Makes 4 servings.

Suggested Wine: Sauvignon Blanc

Now, you might think that by spending so much money on the recovery of these trashfish, the FWS is trying to redress their "previous sins". However, in an ironic and somewhat perverse twist, because the squawfish do attack young trout and salmon, the FWS are actually paying fishermen $3 for every squawfish they catch that measures more than 11 inches!

FILLETS OF CHUB ORLY

The term Orly, in French cooking terminology, is applied to skinned fillets of fish dipped in batter and fried in deep fat, usually served with tomato sauce.

8 fillets of chub, $\frac{1}{4}$ lb. each   2 T chopped parsley
1 teaspoon salt   dipping batter for
$\frac{1}{4}$ t ground pepper   frying fish
$1\frac{1}{2}$ T lemon juice   any homemade
                                tomato sauce

Marinate the fillets 1 hour in the salt, pepper, lemon juice, and parsley. Dip the fish in dipping batter and fry until browned in deep fat preheated to 375° F. Drain on paper towels. Serve hot, with tomato sauce in a separate bowl. Makes 4 servings.

Suggested beverage: Pale Ale or Lager

Some possible substitutions: Apache trout, Borax Lake chub, Chihuahua chub, Chinook salmon, Coho salmon, Gila trout, Greenback cutthroat trout, Hutton tui chub, Lahontan cutthroat trout, Little Kern golden trout, Mojave tui chub, Owens tui chub, Pahranagat roundtail chub, Paiute cutthroat trout, Slender chub, Snake River sockeye salmon, Sonora chub, Spotfin chub, Virgin River chub, Yaqui catfish, Yaqui chub.

Golden-Cheeked Warbler
Dendroica chrysoparia

Marj and Roger Krueger are typical victims of the Endangered Species Act. After paying $53,000 for their one-and-a-half acre lot in Austin, Texas, the Kruegers were restricted from building their dream house by the FWS. Although there are no endangered species on their property, the Golden-cheeked warbler was sighted in "the canyon adjacent" to their property. "The irony," according to Ms Krueger in a *Wall Street Journal* article, "is that the lot itself has only one tree on it, and it's a scrub. We were going to cut that one down and put 20 trees up."

GOLDEN-CHEEKED WARBLER NORMANDY

6 Golden-cheeked warblers	6 red apples
2 T butter	$\frac{1}{2}$ cup chicken stock
$\frac{1}{2}$ cup cider	$\frac{1}{2}$ cup cream
$\frac{1}{4}$ cup white wine	

Pluck, singe and draw the warblers, keeping the giblets. Peel, core and slice the apples and sauté the slices for a few moments in butter. Line a baking dish with the sautéed apples, add the stock and cider, then the minced giblets and the warblers. Cook in a rather fast oven for 20 minutes or until the birds are tender. Pour off the stock, leaving the apple slices and warblers. In a separate saucepan, mix (without boiling) the stock with the cream and white wine. Pour this mixture over the warblers and serve in the same dish. Serves 2-3.

Suggested wine: Retsina

The Kruegers are not the only people of Travis County, Texas to be financially affected by the Endangered Species Act. According to the county's Deputy Chief Tax Appraiser, the listing of the golden-cheeked warbler and the black-capped vireo, and the subsequent land use restrictions, plummeted county property values by nearly $360 million. Before the two songbirds were added to the endangered species list, the market appraisal of this real estate was ten times greater than after the listing.

Approximately 13,000 pairs of these neotropical birds breed in stands of mature ash-junipers (locally called cedars), mixed with oak and elm, on 300,000 to 500,000 acres across thirty-three counties in Central Texas. The US Fish and Wildlife Service listed the golden-cheeked warbler as endangered in 1990, and in 1994 considered designating as many as 800,000 acres as "critical habitat" in order to protect the warbler everywhere in its breeding range. Section 7 of the Endangered Species Act prevents owners of critical habitat from obtaining federally backed loans, insurance, water and sewage hookups, and many times even maintenance of public roads running through their land.

However, for political reasons, and pressure from then-Texas Governor Ann Richards and the Clinton Administration, Interior Secretary Bruce Babbitt said the agency will "cease work" on the critical habitat designation and will "direct their energies towards working with the State, local governments, property owners and other interested citizens to establish habitat conservation plans that protect our natural heritage and our economic potential." Giving back the authority to the states and local governments as well as private property owners is a step in the right direction, however it may be a bit too late for the Kruegers.

GOLDEN-CHEEKED WARBLER ON TOAST

12 golden-cheeked warblers	Dijon mustard
Salt and ground pepper	1 t crushed thyme
6 slices lean bacon	2 onions, sliced
12 slices toasted bread	Butter
2 tablespoons Dijon mustard	Lemon wedges

Preheat oven to 425°F. Rub cleaned warblers, split lengthwise with salt, freshly ground pepper, Dijon mustard, and crushed thyme. Wrap half a slice of bacon around each bird. Place birds in a baking pan over a bed of sliced onions.

Roast warblers 15 minutes. Remove birds from baking pan and place under a hot broiler for 5 minutes. Discard bacon.   ☞

Butter toast and spread Dijon mustard over each slice. Serve warblers over toast with sour cream sauce and lemon wedges. Serves 4-6.

Suggested beverage: Champagne and Orange Juice

It may also be too late for developer David Trotter. After satisfying all state and local zoning requirements to develop his property on Canyon Creek near Austin, Texas, Trotter was blatantly blackmailed by the FWS to develop a public warbler refuge without compensation.

Mr. Trotter's property not only hosts golden-cheeked warblers, but also apparently contains Tooth Cave Ground Beetles, Kretschmarr Cave Mold Beetles, Tooth Cave Pseudoscorpions, Tooth Cave Spiders, and possibly even Bone Cave Harvestmen and Black-capped Vireos. Consequently, the FWS demanded that Trotter "convey through donation to an appropriate entity approved by the Service" 721 acres of his land "to ensure that it is protected in perpetuity."

In addition, the FWS requires "reasonable and prudent measures necessary and appropriate to minimize incidental take of warblers." This includes "(1) [that Trotter] acquire and donate to an appropriate entity an additional 873 acres of land in the Bull Creek, Cypress Creek, or North Lake Austin watersheds for the warblers; and (2) contribute operation and maintenance funds for the 873-acre warbler preserve to an appropriate entity approved by the Service." A total of 1,594 privately owned acres of land without compensation for a public refuge. If that isn't a Government "taking", I don't know what is.

Some possible substitutions: Bachman's wood warbler, Kirtland's warbler, Nightingale reed warbler, Wood warbler.

Grizzly Bear
Ursus arctos horribilis

In the case of Christy v. Hodel, the Endangered Species Act's prohibition of "taking" forbade Richard P. Christy to disturb grizzly bears that were killing his sheep. Apparently, according to the courts, he was supposed to provide sustenance, as well as habitat, for the "endangered" bear. Mr. Christy appealed his case to the US Supreme Court, which refused to hear it. However, in a dissenting statement, Justice Byron White wrote, "A man's right to defend his property has long been recognized at common law...Perhaps a Government edict barring one from resisting the loss of his property is the constitutional equivalent of taking such property in the first place." Subsequently, Mr. Christy was forced to abandon his sheep-ranching practice.

GRIZZLY BEAR LOIN STEAKS

2 loin steaks, $2\frac{1}{2}$ lb.,   2 t lemon juice
      $\frac{5}{8}$"-$\frac{3}{4}$" thick $1\frac{1}{4}$ t salt
1 T butter, melted $\frac{1}{2}$ cup boiling
ground pepper   water

Wipe steaks clean with a damp cloth. Trim off all the fat because it is strong flavored. This leaves about $1\frac{1}{2}$ lbs. lean steak. Place steak on a hot, greased broiler rack set 4 inches from heat. Combine butter and lemon juice and brush over top of steaks. Sprinkle with half of the salt and pepper. Broil 4 to 5 minutes. Turn steaks, brush with remaining lemon-butter and remaining salt and pepper. Broil another 4 or 5 minutes for med-rare steaks. Remove from broiler to platter. Drizzle $\frac{1}{2}$ cup water over rack and scrape down the residue into the drip pan. Remove rack. Stir gravy until well blended; reheat to boiling. Pour over hot steaks and serve immediately. 4 to 5 servings.

Suggested Wine: Cabernet Sauvignon

In the most far reaching endangered species decision yet, the court ruled that a citizen does not even have the right to defend his own life from attack by an endangered species.

Montana sheep rancher, John Shuler, was tending to his sheep, when three bears attacked his flock, some 30 feet away from him. Shuler fired a warning shot to frighten them off, when suddenly, out of the darkness, a fourth bear turned to attack him. He shot the bear.

The next morning, expecting to find the bear dead, Shuler was startled as the bear reared up on its hind legs and charged toward him. Fearing for his life, Shuler shot the bear again. The bear got up again and Shuler fired another shot, this time killing the bear.

The Interior Department fined Shuler $7,000 for "taking" the bear in violation of the Endangered Species Act. Despite Shuler's argument that killing the bear was allowable under the act's self-defense clause, a judge ordered him to pay a reduced fine of $4,000.

Some possible substitutions: Louisiana black bear.

California Gnatcatcher
Polioptila californica californica

Much has been discussed about "ecosystem management", whereby areas are set aside to protect a myriad of species rather than the protection of individual species. In Southern California, the State, with a group of scientists, is trying to develop just such a plan. The plan touted by Interior Secretary Bruce Babbitt as "breathtaking" is called the Natural Communities Conservation Plan (NCCP), introduced in 1991. The first pilot plan was to develop a conservation plan for the coastal-sage-scrub ecosystem scattered across 6,000 square miles in five Southern California counties. This scrub is home to the California gnatcatcher, and also happens to be some of the most expensive and sought after real estate in the country.

As the NCCP was being studied, developers "voluntarily" idled 200,000 privately owned acres, where land prices range from $150,000 to $500,000, and even as high as $3-million per acre. Their good-faith effort was made on the belief that by working within the system and under the maxim of compromise, the Government would hold off listing the gnatcatcher as a threatened species. In this way, the pro-active habitat-conservation plans, would allow property owners to set aside habitat for rare animals, birds and plants in exchange for approval to build on the rest of their land. A balance between competing concerns for jobs and the environment. A development that is in the best interest of species and land owners alike.

ROAST GNATCATCHER

8 young gnatcatchers   1 cup corn oil
$\frac{1}{2}$ teaspoon black pepper   1 onion, quartered
1 apple, quartered $\frac{1}{4}$ cup hot water
8 cooking cloths, soaked in corn oil

Preheat oven to 375° F.

    Brush each gnatcatcher with corn oil and sprinkle with pepper. Place onion and apple pieces in each gnatcatcher. Place gnatcatchers in roasting pan and place in oven. Immediately reduce heat to 300° F and roast until lightly browned, about 15 minutes.

    Cover each gnatcatcher with a cooking cloth soaked with corn oil. Add the hot water, poured around sides. Cover and continue to roast for 45 minutes or until tender. Baste often and add more corn oil as necessary. Remove cooking cloths for last 10 minutes.

    When done, discard onion and apple pieces. Serve with pan gravy and boiled potatoes. Serves 4.

Suggested wine: Chardonnay

However, armed with unsubstantiated "scientific" data, the Natural Resources Defense Council petitioned the US Fish and Wildlife Service to have the California gnatcatcher listed as endangered. Without allowing public review of the data used to "justify" its listing, the California gnatcatcher was listed as threatened on March 25, 1993.

Now this listing was not one of your typical listings (and then again, maybe it was). It seems the lead witness of the NRDC at the hearings held by Fish and Wildlife was the "expert" on gnatcatchers. Through his extensive studies in the 1970's and 1980's, Dr. Jonathan Atwood had determined that there were two species of gnatcatchers, *Polioptila californica californica* and *P.c. margaritae*. The two separate subspecies were differentiated by their calls, although they are almost identical in appearance. *P. c. margaitae* live in Mexico and the Southwestern United States, while the *P.c. californica* resides primarily in Baja California with an offshoot population in Southern California. Neither subspecies is threatened or endangered, with populations of *P.c. californica* reaching as high as 1.5 to 2.0 million throughout its entire range.

However, during the listing hearings, Dr. Atwood appended his original study, and declared a third subspecies, *P.c. abbreviata*, based on plumage coloration without adjusting for age differences, and that *P.c. californica* resided north of the 30° North Latitude line crossing northern Baja California. By designating an "offshoot population" as a subspecies, the population of breeding pairs was reduced remarkably. Atwood, and the NRDC, submitted that there were only 2500 pairs in southern California and 2500 pairs in northern Baja. When pressed for the statistical data used to come to these conclusions, Dr. Atwood refused, and later said his original records had been destroyed. Subsequently, numerous biologists and biostatisticians have been unable to come to the same empirical findings as Dr. Atwood. Their findings, in fact, after adjusting for age differences, clearly show that there is no break in the populations of gnatcatchers at 30° N. Latitude, and the range of *P. californica* extends to 25° N. Latitude.

A Federal judge, Judge Stanley Sporkin, subsequently ruled that the US Fish and Wildlife Service violated provisions of the Endangered Species Act by not providing the public enough access to data used to determine that the non-descript songbird was imperiled, and set aside the listing of the gnatcatcher. After the May 2, 1994 decision by Judge Sporkin, Dr. Atwood released his research, with admitted changes in data and empirical values. Since that time, developers and private landowners have turned their efforts and energy back to developing multiple species habitat conservation plans, and the US Fish and Wildlife Service re-listed the California gnatcatcher as a threatened species. Additionally the NRDC has filed yet another suit to de-rail the multiple species plans even before they are complete, to force even larger dedications of land without regard to private property rights or economic considerations. They want to go back to "protecting every bird in every bush."

ITALIAN GNATCATCHER

8 gnatcatchers	8 large pitted olives
8 small artichokes hearts in oil	1 cup breadcrumbs
$1\frac{1}{2}$ cups dry white wine	8 pinches of oregano
1 clove garlic	$\frac{1}{2}$ cup olive oil
Salt and ground pepper	

Drain the oil from artichoke hearts and save the oil. In a saucepan place the wine and artichoke hearts, bring to a boil and immediately remove from heat. Remove and cool the hearts of artichoke.

Rub the inside of eight gnatcatchers with salt and pepper, push one large pitted olive into the cavity of each bird, followed with an artichoke heart and plug with browned breadcrumbs slightly moistened with wine. Rub the birds outside, thoroughly, with the oil from the artichoke hearts supplemented by $\frac{1}{2}$ cup of olive oil. Place in a roasting pan, put a pinch of oregano over each breast, split a clove of garlic and put it in the bottom of the roasting pan. Put it all into a preheated 450°F oven for 5 minutes.

Meanwhile add the remainder of the olive oil to the saucepan of white wine. After 5 minutes reduce the oven to 300°F, and, basting frequently with wine-oil mixture, cook for another 15 minutes or until birds are tender. Remove to serving platter and eat immediately. Serve with saffron rice, baked zucchini squash and a tossed green salad. Serves 4.

Suggested wine: Chenin Blanc

One developer who was caught with gnatcatcher habitat was John Barone. Barone, a senior project manager for the Fieldstone Company, a large home builder, was faced with the prospect of how to deal with the California gnatcatcher on his 2300 undeveloped acres of land in northern San Diego County. The land near the La Costa golf course and resort, purchased in 1988 for $180 million, was to house some 3,000 upper-middle-class homes. When 100 of the small song birds were discovered on his property, and well before their listing as threatened, he met with consultants, environmentalists, city and county officials, and Fish and Wildlife biologists, to help design a habitat plan that would pre-empt the Government from shutting down his project.

After hammering out many proposals, altering lot lines and re-designing much of the project, the parties came to a plan that would be acceptable to FWS. The final plan finally presented would cost Barone about $12 million and block development on 500 acres. In return, Fieldstone would be able to develop the remaining 1400 acres of buildable land.

Celebration was short lived for Barone and the Fieldstone Company, however. Fish and Wildlife let Barone know that on the acreage on which he was allowed to build (because he set aside land for the gnatcatcher), were Del Mar Manzanita, a soon to be listed endangered species. And that there were thirty-six potentially listable species known to live on his land, and another 30 that "might someday take up residence there". Setting out to modify his habitat-conservation plan yet another time, Barone decided to deal with each and every species.

A habitat conservation plan was finally approved, and Barone was finally granted permits to develop his land. He ended up setting aside 700 acres of land for habitat on-site, and buying and setting aside another 240 acres off-site.

This kind of project-by-project and species-by-species habitat-conservation planning has been called the "species of the month club" by other developers, and they intend to continue to develop a master conservation plan that will set the rules for an entire region.   The NCCP would accomplish those goals that eliminate a patchwork of habitats and develop manageable ecosystems,   a concept long fought for by mainstream environmentalists.   However, it seems some extremists groups that continually file lawsuits against any and all ecosystem plans are maybe just trying to perpetuate their own existence.   Every lawsuit,   no matter how ill-conceived,   brings in those much needed donations.

Some possible substitutions: See Black-capped vireo, Golden-cheeked warbler, Grasshopper sparrow.

Grasshopper Sparrow
Ammodramus savannarum floridanus

This sparrow is found in the interior of Florida in the Kissimmee Valley spread through a five county area.   Their habitat is low-growing native plants up to 18 inches high.   Like most other species, it moves to desired habitat quite frequently. There is a large public land mass that is managed by the Government and leaseholders in the valley to provide appropriate habitat.   In other words,   they must chop or burn to keep vegetation from becoming to thick or high.

A rancher in the Kissimmee Valley wanted to convert some overgrown range pasture into citrus.   Federal agencies required that prior to clearing and planting citrus,   biological studies be conducted to prove there were no grasshopper sparrow flocks in the overgrown area.   Now, mind you, this study was required even though the habitat was overgrown and not suitable for the species,   and the species is mobile and would willingly move to a new site if disrupted.

The landowner had to hire a biologist and provide several of his own employees to conduct this survey.   It cost him thousands of dollars and a substantial delay, just to prove that there were no grasshopper sparrows on this site with undesirable habitat. The only reason for the survey, was that the land was in the Kissimmee Valley,   the grasshopper sparrow's designated range.

GRASSHOPPER SPARROW PIE

6 large grasshopper sparrows	2 T chopped parsley
1 teaspoon salt	2 T chopped celery
$\frac{1}{4}$ t ground pepper	2 T flour
4 T butter	2 T chopped onions
8 cloves	1 carrot, sliced
Plain pie crust	

Dress wash and dry grasshopper sparrows. Tie legs and wings tight against body. Sprinkle with salt and pepper. Melt 2 tablespoons butter in pan and sauté sparrows, searing thoroughly on all sides. Cover with water. Add onions, cloves, carrots, parsley, and celery. Cover and simmer until tender, about 2 hours. Remove sparrows and separate meat from bones. Mix flour to a smooth paste with balance of melted butter, and stir into pan liquid, bringing to a boil. Line a greased baking dish with pie crust. Put in sparrow meat. Pour in liquid. Cover with pie crust. Bake in hot oven (450° F.) until brown. Serve hot. Serves 4.

Suggested Wine: Sauvignon Blanc

Some possible substitutions: Cape Sable seaside sparrow, Dusky seaside sparrow, Piping plover, Snowy plover, Ponape mountain starling, San Clemente sage sparrow.

Florida Scrub Jay
Aphelocoma coerulescens coerulscens

The Scrub Jay is a calm, docile bird found along the deep sand ridge backbone of Florida. Although state and federal public lands throughout the central ridge contain the scrub habitat that supports the scrub jay, private landowners, including citrus growers, along the central ridge are prohibited from clearing or thinning vegetation from the land.

Farmers in this region find it necessary to hire a biologist to survey their land to assure no scrub jays exist, prior to any normal pasture renovation. And as a defensive measure, citrus growers, after their groves were frozen in the mid-1980's, continued to mow their land so that the scrub plant would not grow back, until they could afford to replant.

MARINATED GRILLED SCRUB JAYS

12 Scrub jays, cleaned and split lengthwise
The Marinade

1 Bottle dry white wine	**1 T wine vinegar**
1 Bay leaf	**2 sprigs fresh thyme**
Salt and pepper	**1 c. chopped celery**
2 cloves garlic, crushed	$\frac{1}{4}$ **lb. butter**

Combine all ingredients for the marinade, and marinate birds in the refrigerator 8 hours. Remove scrub jays from marinade, rinse, and pat dry. (Discard marinade or place in the freezer for a second use.)

Place birds, cut side down, on an oiled barbecue grill in a kettle style barbecue set up for in-direct cooking. Cook over a drip pan for about 20 minutes or until browned, turning from time to time and basting with melted butter.

Serve with French bread, Chinese bean sprouts, and a good bottle of white wine. Serves 4.

Suggested wine: French Colombard

In 1991, over 500 private property owners in Polk and Highlands counties were contacted by the Fish and Wildlife Service and told they must prove they have no scrub jays or potential habitat on their land if they want to clear it of any scrub vegetation. They were warned that "any activity that destroys scrub occupied by scrub jays may violate the Act." Such a violation can result in up to a year in jail and $25,000 (civil) or

$50,000 (criminal) in fines per incident. Furthermore, landowners must prove that there were no scrub jays on their land for the past five years. The cost of meeting this requirement, with the assistance of an environmental consultant, can cost as much as $20,000.

Private property owners have little recourse, if any, if they desire to clear scrub brush from their backyards. And even if they are prohibited from any type of property modification or use, the property owner is still responsible for any and all property taxes. State and Government agency expenditure on the scrub jay have exceeded $20 million to date, and FWS is planning to acquire 12,000 acres of privately held land to form a refuge for the bird.

Some possible substitutions: Crested honeycreeper, Everglade snail kite, large Kauai thrush, Masked bobwhite, Molokai thrush, small Kauai thrush, Yellow shouldered blackbird.

Tulare Pseudobahia Plant
Pseudobahia peirsonii

A cattle rancher in Kern County, California, Mark Melbane, was involved in an eminent domain lawsuit with the Fresno Flood Control District over this endangered plant. The Fresno Flood Control District learned that its $65 million flood control project would damage the plant's habitat, and was ordered to mitigate. They were required to find alternate habitat for the plant in order to be allowed to continue with their project. When they learned that the plant was growing on Melbane's property, they determined that his was the best site for mitigation. They attempted to buy 40 acres of his property, but because it was in the middle of his ranch, he refused to sell.

The District then proceeded to purchase the land through eminent domain, and Melbane fought this procedure, fearing that if his family ever decided to sell the ranch his father had built, it would be difficult at best. The case went all the way to the California Supreme Court, which held for the rancher, but his legal fees were well over $100,000, which he has no way of recovering.

Northern Spotted Owl
Strix occidentalis caurina

Probably no "endangered species" has achieved so much notoriety as has the Northern Spotted Owl, nor has any listing been so hypocritical and unjustified. As Andy Stahl of the Sierra Club Legal Defense Fund stated, "The Northern Spotted Owl is the wildlife species of choice to act as a surrogate for old growth protection." And Randall O'Toole, who describes himself as an "eco-activist", is quoted in *Newsweek* as saying, "Cumulatively, the environmental movement is interested in shutting down the timber industry." Period.

The Northern Spotted Owl, however, is not a species at all, but at best a subspecies of the much larger group of spotted or barred owls, *Strix occidentalis*. Even this is doubtful, since DNA tests fail to show any genetic differences between Northern and Californian spotted owls, or any significant difference with Mexican spotted owls.

The range of spotted owls reaches from British Columbia to Southern California and on into Mexico as far as Mexico City, and eastward to the western edge of Texas. In Washington, the spotted owl is also found in significant numbers east of the Cascades. The greatest concentration of nesting pairs of Northern Spotted Owls is not found in an old growth forest, but a privately owned tree farm in eastern Washington where the oldest trees are 40 years old.

FRICASSEE OF SPOTTED OWL
ROMAN STYLE

1 3-pound Spotted owl   2 T olive oil
3 cloves garlic, crushed   2 t marjoram
1 cup red wine   1 14 oz. can arti-
2 cups soup stock   choke hearts,
$\frac{1}{2}$ cup chopped pancetta   drained
1 cup chopped ripe tomatoes   1 T each butter &
Salt and ground pepper to taste   flour, cooked

    Dress, singe, wash and dry Spotted owl. Cut
into 8 pieces. Heat a large frying pan and add the
oil. Brown the owl pieces well. Remove to a 6-quart
covered stove-top casserole. Add the garlic to the
pan and sauté just a moment. Add red wine to the
pan and heat, then add to the casserole. Add all
remaining ingredients except the artichokes, butter
and flour roux, and salt and pepper. Bring to a boil
and cover. Lower heat to a simmer and cook for 40
minutes. Add the artichokes, quartered, and simmer
another 10 minutes, uncovered. Stir in the roux and
taste for seasoning. Careful with the salt as the
pancetta is salty itself. Serves 4.

Suggested Wine: Gamay Beaujolais

Spotted owls do not build their own nests. They use stick piles, snags with protected cavities or other tree deformities, and abandoned nests. They also will use artificial nesting boxes to raise their young even when natural nesting sites are available. They feed on mammals 90% of the time, preferring wood rats, brush rabbits and flying squirrels, none of which are dependent on old growth forests. They are most often disturbed by natural predators and competitors such as great horned owls and ravens, and are known to thrive in second growth forests that have been harvested and replanted. In fact, in 1987 researchers for the USFWS discovered spotted owls living year round in foothill canyons filled with oaks and sycamores, not the high altitude conifer forests they are supposedly dependent upon.

In 1986, a National Audubon Society committee of owl "experts" concluded that policy should preserve "a minimum of 1500 pairs of spotted owls" in Oregon, Washington, and California. Four years later, the FWS recovery team advocated a recovery plan to protect 2300 pairs. Today, scientists know, through a substantial increase in survey efforts, both private and Government, more than 10,000 owls exist throughout the Pacific Northwest. More than double what it was determined was necessary for a stable and increasing population, and almost five times as many owls as was said to exist when it was listed. And the number continues to increase.

STUFFED SPOTTED OWL

1 Spotted owl	$\frac{1}{2}$ cup ground ham
2 Tablespoons lemon juice	$\frac{1}{3}$ cup chopped
Salt and ground pepper	almonds
12 chicken livers, cut in half	$\frac{1}{2}$ t dried thyme
4 T butter	8 slices bacon
$\frac{2}{3}$ cup chopped mushrooms	Watercress

☞

Rub the inside of the body cavity of the dressed owl with 1 tablespoon of the lemon juice and

salt and black pepper. Cook the chicken livers
(along with the owl liver) in a skillet in 2
tablespoons of the butter until barely done. Transfer
them to a wooden bowl and chop them fine. In the
same skillet, sauté the mushrooms in the remaining
2 tablespoons butter. Add this to the livers, along
with the ham, almonds and thyme. Season to taste
with salt and ground pepper. Stuff the mixture
lightly into the body cavity of the Spotted owl. Close
the opening with skewers and lace them tightly with
twine. Tie the legs together. Rub the skin with the
remaining 1 tablespoon lemon juice and salt and
pepper. Place the owl on a rack, breast side up, in a
shallow baking pan. Cover the breast with thin
slices of bacon. Roast in a preheated slow oven (325°
F.) 1 hour, or until owl is done, basting occasionally
with pan drippings. Serve hot or cold, garnished
with watercress. Serves 4.

Suggested Wine: Chardonnay

As was mentioned earlier, there is approximately 730
million acres of forest land in the United States. That represents
32% of the entire land mass, and is two-thirds of what existed in
1600. Roughly 483 million acres is considered commercial forest
land, 72% of which is privately owned (15% owned by forest
products companies and 57% owned by private individuals). Of
the 28% of commercial forest that is publicly owned, 18% is in
national forests and 10% in other federal and state ownership. Of
the national forests, only 42% was harvestable prior to the listing
of the Northern Spotted Owl, and the majority of that has now
been placed off limits. Overall across the west, federal forests
provided 44 percent of the timber processed into lumber in 1990,
and in 1994 they furnished only 17 percent of the resource. And
because of the listing of the Mexican spotted owl (*Strix
occidentalis lucida*) in March 1993, logging has been halted on
all national forests in Arizona and New Mexico, along with all
Navajo Indian lands in the Southwest, as well.

It doesn't take a rocket scientist to realize that future wood products are going to have to come from foreign soil or private lands. But what of the spotted owl on private property? Well, ask Betty Orem. Betty Orem isn't exactly what you would call a timber baron. She owns 27 acres of tall trees adjoining the Olympic National Forest. Since her father bought the stand in 1928, the family has used it mainly for firewood and sometimes for timber.

In 1989 some of Orem's trees were accidentally damaged by Forest Service logging nearby. When she sought compensation, the Forest Service said she needed to harvest and sell the damaged trees for their salvage value. She applied for a permit to cut them, but had trouble getting one because a spotted owl had nested a half-mile away in the national forest.

RASPBERRY-GLAZED SPOTTED OWL

$\frac{1}{2}$ lb. pork sausage w/o casing	4 T unsalted butter
4 green onions, chopped	$\frac{1}{2}$ cup toasted,
$\frac{1}{3}$ lb. Gruyere cheese, grated	chopped almonds
1 Spotted owl	$\frac{3}{4}$ cup stuffing mix
2 T olive oil	2 T raspberry
2 T raspberry jam	vinegar

Sauté sausage in butter until just done (6 to 8) minutes. Add green onions and cook an additional minute. Drain grease and transfer mixture to a large bowl and add almonds, cheese, and stuffing mix. Thoroughly chill stuffing mix. Wash owl and pat dry. When stuffing is well chilled, stuff and truss the bird. In a small bowl combine olive oil, vinegar and jam to form a glaze. Rub owl thoroughly with this mixture and reserve remaining glaze.   ☞

Prepare fire in kettle style barbecue for indirect-heat method of cooking. When fire is ready, place owl in the center of oiled grill over a drip pan. Cover with lid. Baste owl several times with reserved glaze during cooking. Cook 45 minutes to 1 hour or until done. Serves 4-6.

Suggested Wine: Pinot Noir

As one of the many private landowners who were plaintiffs in the Sweet Home Chapter of Communities for a Greater Oregon v. Bruce Babbitt, Secretary of the Interior, Orem was relieved when the Appellate Court ruled. The Court held that the original framers of the Endangered Species Act, did not intend for the FWS to have such broad and inflexible powers as to halt the economic livelihood of private individuals and small communities. However, her relief was short lived, when the US Supreme Court reversed that finding saying it was not their place to interpret the intent of the authors, and gave the Interior Department, and thus FWS, unlimited, unrestricted, and unbridled power over private land.

Now the Government has dictated that 5700 acres must be kept as "suitable habitat" surrounding each nesting pair of owls. In this case, they have virtually shut down 5 million acres of timber land, 40% of which is privately owned and over 50% of that is owned by individuals with less than 300 acre parcels. Including Betty Orem's 27 acre plot.

CHINESE SMOKED SPOTTED OWL

It is always a good idea to make more than one bird when using this recipe since there is little additional work involved. The owl is delicious cold in Chinese Smoked-Owl Salad, so use two Spotted owls. Extra leftovers are good to have. ☞

Brine

1 gallon water	$1\frac{1}{2}$ cup kosher salt
1 cup sugar	$\frac{1}{2}$ cup soy sauce
1 t Chinese five-spice powder	2 slices fresh ginger

Cure

Wash dressed Spotted owls thoroughly inside and out. Place owls in a large non-aluminum, non-cast iron container, cover with well mixed and dissolved brine, and weigh birds down with heavy plate so they stay submerged. Refrigerate 16 to 20 hours. Remove from brine and reserve brine. Wash owls and pat dry.

Smoke Cooking

2 Cured Spotted owls	1 t Chinese five-
1 ginger root (about $\frac{1}{4}$ lb.) sliced $\frac{1}{4}$" thick slices	spice powder
6 Whole star anise, soaked in water for 30 minutes	

Sprinkle cavities of each washed owl with Chinese five-spice powder. Prepare water smoker for smoke cooking. (2 layers of charcoal and 6 to 8 chunks of oak, mesquite or apple wood). Put 2 cups of reserved brine in the pan, then fill the pan with hot water. Place owls breast side up on the grill. Cover and smoke cook at a temperature between 200° F and 250° F. Add charcoal, wood, and water as needed. Check the internal temperature of the owls after about 3 hours. When it reaches 150° F, add the ginger root and star anise to the coals. The owls are done when the internal temperature reaches 160° F to 165° F (about 4 to $4\frac{1}{2}$ hours of cooking). Remove owls from smoker. Let rest 10 minutes before cutting into quarters with poultry shears and serving. Serves 4.

Suggested Beverage: Chinese Beer (Tsing Tao, etc.) or Plum Wine

If each pair of nesting owls supposedly needs 5700 acres around each nest, and there are 4,000 known pairs (a figure that is increasing almost daily) then there will have to be an additional 22,800,000 acres of valuable timber land, mostly private, set idle. And with 10,000 known owls (a figure that is also increasing at a rapid rate) the nesting pairs could increase even faster.

ROAST OWL BREAST IN ORANGE SAUCE

4 Whole Spotted owl breasts	4 T olive oil
2 Oranges, juiced	1 T watercress
Salt and pepper to taste	$\frac{1}{4}$ cup warm water

Split the Spotted owl down the backbone (legs and wings removed) and flatten without separating. Heat 1 tablespoon of the olive oil in a heavy skillet. Very lightly brown the skin on the meaty sides of the breasts. Remove breasts from the skillet and brush both sides with the remaining olive oil. Place bony side up in roasting pan. Roast, uncovered, for 20 minutes in pre-heated oven at 375° F.

Remove from oven and turn breasts meaty side up. Reduce oven heat to 300° F. Pour orange juice over breasts, and add watercress. Cover, return to oven and roast for 45 minutes, basting twice.

Remove from oven and sprinkle with salt and pepper. Add warm water around sides to increase moisture as needed. Return to oven and roast, uncovered, and additional 20 minutes, basting once.

Remove Spotted owl from roasting pan and place on serving platter. Pour pan juices over the owl. Serve with sweet potatoes and cranberry sauce. Serves 4.

Suggested wine: Fume Blanc

Does it benefit a landowner to produce habitat for the spotted owl? Well, Simpson Timber, a private timber company has done such a good job in managing their commercial forest in the redwood region of California, they found and banded 603 spotted owls. This land is primarily plantation young growth on a 40 to 60-year rotation, but because of the spotted owl, Simpson had to idle some 50,000 acres of their own land.

Every timber company, every county and community, and every private land owner that has timber or a timber related business, large and small, in the three state area of the Northern Spotted Owl habitat, has been adversely affected by this listing. And as was the case of Betty Orem, an owl doesn't have to land on your property. In 1993 the federal Government filed an enforcement action to halt Anderson and Middleton from harvesting timber on 72 acres of private land on Washington's Olympic Peninsula. The reason for this action was, you guessed it, a pair of spotted owls nesting. Not on Anderson and Middleton's 72-acre plot, mind you, but on Government land a full 1.6 miles away.

Habitat Conservation Plans, or HCP's, are becoming a way of dealing with the stringent regulations of the Endangered Species Act for some large companies. The Murray Pacific Corp. in Mineral, Washington had spent over $650,000 during the late 1980's and early 1990's, developing a plan to protect the three spotted owls found on their 53,527-acre tree farm on the slopes of the Cascades. After two years of being idled because of these three owls, Murray Pacific was ready to start harvesting again. Then the their worst nightmare was realized. A marbled murrelet was spotted on their property

"We hadn't even broken out the champagne when a marbled murrelet dipped its wing over the west end of the tree farm," company Vice President Toby Murray recalled.

In order to protect their land, Murray Pacific Corp. signed a Habitat Conservation Plan with the US Fish and Wildlife Service. It is an all-species protection plan that will guarantee over the next 100 years a measure of safe habitat not only for the owls and the murrelets, but for any red-legged frogs, eagles, goshawks, wolves, bears, big eared bats or at least 28 other endangered or threatened species that might venture onto Murray Pacific forest.

In exchange for a broad array of protection measures, the Federal Government has pledged to guarantee continued logging operations, even if a new and previously unrecognized endangered species shows up. These Habitat Conservation Plans, seem to be a way for Secretary of the Interior, Bruce Babbitt, to ward off the ever increasing hostility to the Endangered Species Act. If the Government stands behind their pledge (big IF), this type of cooperation between Government and large companies may go along way to ease the burdens imposed by the ESA. But what of the small guy? Murray Pacific Corp. estimates the cost of these protection measures will cost the company over $100 million over the next 50 years.

Some possible substitutions: Attwater's greater prairie chicken, Boreal owl, Hawaiian common moorhen, Mariana common moorhen, Mexican spotted owl.

Salt Marsh Harvest Mouse
Reithrodontomys raviventris
California Clapper Rail
Rallus longirostris obsoletus

The Shorelands Company wanted to build a race track and industrial park on a 740-acre parcel known as the Baumberg Tract at the southern end of the San Francisco Bay. The property is the site of a former salt harvesting facility and is characterized by salt laden clays that are barren, sterile, and support no vegetation. The US Fish and Wildlife Service argued that development on this site would endanger the Salt Marsh Harvest Mouse and the California Clapper Rail, even though these species have not been found on the property. Both species depend on dense stands of pickleweed and cord grass found in tidal salt marshes. There is, by there own admission, no suitable habitat on the property for either species, nor is there any prospect that suitable habitat could develop naturally.

The FWS offered a number of changes Shorelands could make, in a future proposal, to prevent jeopardizing the species which are not on the property, yet stated that even if they were all included in a future proposal, they would still oppose the project.

SALT MARSH HARVEST MOUSE STEW

3-4 dressed harvest mice	1 cup bouillon
1 teaspoon salt	1 cup dry white wine
$\frac{1}{2}$ t ground pepper	12 pearl onions
flour	3 T butter
3-4 T bacon drippings	8 new potatoes
$\frac{3}{4}$ t chopped garlic	chopped parsley

Cut the mice into serving-size pieces, rub with $\frac{1}{2}$ t of salt and $\frac{1}{4}$ teaspoon of black pepper, and dredge with flour. Brown on all sides in 3 tablespoons of the bacon drippings. Add the garlic, bouillon and wine. Cover, and simmer 1 hour. Brown the onions in 2 T of the butter and add to the mice, along with the potatoes and $\frac{1}{2}$ t salt and $\frac{1}{4}$ t black pepper. Cover and cook 30 minutes or until mice and vegetables are tender. Transfer the mice and vegetables to a warmed serving dish. Blend 1T flour with the remaining 1 T butter to form a roux. Add to the liquid, mix well, and cook until the sauce bubbles. Pour over the mice. Sprinkle with chopped parsley.

Suggested Wine: Merlot

So, why is Fish and Wildlife so opposed to this project, even though they argue that any efforts at habitat restoration would be doomed to failure? It turns out, that FWS has their eyes on acquiring the property themselves. Certainly, developable property in an urban area like San Francisco that might command a six figure price per acre would be cheaper for FWS to "acquire" if nobody else were allowed to do anything with the property.

Subsequently, the Shorelands Company, after spending $12 million on this project, to find out it can't do anything with the property because of two endangered species that aren't there, filed bankruptcy.

SMOTHERED CALIFORNIA CLAPPER RAIL

Clapper rail wings and legs are best used for stock, if at all. They are much tougher than the breast meat, even in the youngest birds, and mainly consist of tendons and inedible membrane. Most people prepare only the breasts for the table.

6 Clapper rail breasts	$\frac{1}{2}$ cup rye flour
$\frac{1}{4}$ cup olive oil	1 large onion, sliced
1 clove garlic, chopped	$1\frac{1}{2}$ c chicken stock
3 celery stalks	2 large carrots
1 cup mushrooms, sliced	$\frac{1}{2}$ c black olives

Place Clapper rail breasts, one at a time, in a paper sack with rye flour. Shake to coat thoroughly. Heat olive oil in a skillet at medium heat, and brown coated breasts. Place browned rail breast in a casserole dish.

Sauté onion, garlic, celery and carrots (sliced in long pieces) in the hot olive oil for 7 minutes. Drain vegetables and distribute over Clapper rail breasts, then pour the chicken stock on top. Bake, uncovered, for $1\frac{1}{2}$ hours at 325° F. Ten minutes before done, add mushrooms and sliced olives. Serves 2.

Suggested wine: California Chardonnay

The same area has been costly to the cities and counties to the south of it, in the name of these two species. It seems that the EPA and the FWS, have limited discharge of treated wastewater by the San Jose-Santa Clara Water Pollution Control Plant into an estuary that spills into the San Francisco Bay. The problem, according to the FWS, is that the wastewater is just too darn clean. Fresh water pumped into the estuary is apparently converting a saltwater marsh into a freshwater marsh.

In order to comply with this reduced discharge, the area's water districts are going to build a maze of nearly 100 miles of distribution pipelines throughout a two county area at a cost of $460 million of taxpayer money.

Some possible substitutions: Alabama beach mouse, Anastasia Island beach mouse, Choctawahatchee beach mouse, Key Largo cotton mouse, Perdido Key beach mouse, Southern beach mouse.
Also: Guam rail, Light-footed clapper rail, Yuma clapper rail.

Delta Smelt
Hypomerus transpacificus

This three inch long nearly translucent fish, that they say smells like a cucumber, and lives for only a year, is the cause of great concern and consternation for the farmers of the agriculturally rich California Central Valley. With its listing as threatened in 1993, part of FWS effort to list an increasing number of species, reduction to the already depleted water supplies to this valley could be devastating. Following six years of drought in California, and reduced flows of water to protect salmon and bass in the Sacramento-San Joaquin Delta, the pumps taking fresh water out of the Delta to irrigate the farms of the valley, and provide drinking water to almost two-thirds of the states inhabitants, have been slowed. Water supplies have already been reduced by 30-40%, and the listing could reduce it by as much as 50% and cost $12 billion in lost business.

DELTA SMELT ANTIPASTI

Wash the smelts and make a slight opening at the gills with a sharp knife. Draw them between the thumb and finger from tail to head to press the intestines out at the gill opening, keeping the fish whole. Wash and pat dry. ☞

1 cup flour, seasoned with salt and pepper	1 Lb. fresh smelts
	1 cup olive oil
$\frac{1}{4}$ cup red-wine vinegar	$\frac{1}{2}$ yellow onion
2 cloves garlic, crushed	1 t dry rosemary
1 t crushed dry sage	$\frac{1}{4}$ c white seedless
$\frac{1}{4}$ c toasted pine nuts	raisins
$\frac{1}{4}$ t dried hot red-pepper flakes	Chopped parsley

Dredge the smelts in the seasoned flour. Pan-fry in $\frac{1}{4}$ cup of the olive oil. Do not overcook; $1\frac{1}{2}$ minutes per side should be ample. Remove to a cooking rack or paper towels.

In a pan sauté the garlic, rosemary, sage, and red-pepper flakes in $\frac{1}{2}$ cup olive oil for just a few moments. Add the wine vinegar and reduce for a couple of minutes. Set aside.

In another pan sauté the onion, sliced thin, in the remaining $\frac{1}{4}$ cup oil until they are soft. Do not brown the onion.

When the smelts are cool, remove the heads and cut lengthwise to debone. Arrange on a platter with the skin side down. Add the sautéed onion, raisins, and pine nuts to the vinegar and herb reduction. Pour all of this over the smelts. Garnish with parsley. Serves 8.

Suggested wine: Grappa

As they say in the valley, on billboards along the major highways, "No water, no farms. No farms, no food. No food, no future." Stephen Hall, executive director of the Association of California Water Agencies, echoes the sentiment of millions of people across the country. "The time has come...to solve problems for endangered species and people at the same time, rather than pitting fish against people in the haphazard and adversarial way we have been doing."

Some possible substitutions: **Ash Meadows speckled dace, Big Spring spinedace, Blackside dace, Blue shiner, Cape Fear shiner, Clover Valley speckled dace, Conasauga logperch, Desert dace, Foskett speckled dace, Independence Valley speckled dace, Kendall Warm Springs dace, Moapa dace, Pecos bluntnose shiner.**

San Marcos Salamander
Eurycea nana

In the Texas "hill country", an area in central Texas extending from Dallas/Fort Worth to the gulf of Mexico, there are wooded canyons and thousands of crystalline springs. Underneath it all are vast honeycombed formations of limestone, where water from the springs and the hills form subterranean rivers, caves and flooded crevices, feed the Edwards Aquifer, the primary water supply for the farmers, ranchers, and over 1.5 million other inhabitants living in the city of San Antonio. In February 1993, the Sierra Club won a suit to force FWS to regulate the pumpage of water from the Edwards Aquifer in order to protect the San Marcos salamander, which inhabits the San Marcos Springs, one of two primary "spill points" of the aquifer. The Government proposed to reduce the water usage in this area by 60%, which would cost taxpayers an estimated $7 billion over the next 20 years.

Failure to comply would, according to FWS, affect all federal programs "from food stamps, federally insured home loans, farm subsidies, grants for police programs, to road construction and job training."

The limestone caves under the surface of the hill country is also home to the Texas blind salamander (*Typhylomolge rathbuni*). In the blackness of these underground caves, the need for site was unnecessary and this salamander, through evolution, got rid of its sight capability. Also, because there is no light, there was no need for color, so the salamander is colorless. The

Texas blind salamander *chose* to live in the eternal darkness of these caves, or was trapped underground by some freak accident of geology, but is it really endangered? Or is it, as some scientist contend, one of the failures of evolution, already doomed before man knew of its existence? Whatever the case, the preservationists are holding this species up as another keystone species of the area in order to halt farming, ranching and development around the Texas hill country.

TEXAS BLIND SALAMANDER SHISH KEBAB

2 Lb.. salamander meat, cut
    into 2-inch cubes
$\frac{1}{2}$ c chopped parsley
$\frac{1}{2}$ cup olive oil
Salt and ground pepper
1 large firm tomato
4 large mushrooms

1 onion, sliced
4 T lemon juice
2 cloves garlic
4 sprigs thyme
$\frac{1}{2}$ t ground cumin
1 large green pepper
3 T heavy cream

Place salamander meat in large bowl. Blend olive oil and lemon juice with all herbs and spices and pour over salamander meat, mixing well. Marinate in refrigerator 24 hours or more, turning meat occasionally.

Remove salamander from marinade, and thread meat and cut vegetables on skewers. Brush salamander with heavy cream. Broil 5 inches from heat, turning the skewers to cook evenly. Broil about 10 to 12 minutes or until vegetables are done. Slide salamander and vegetables off the skewers and onto a bed of rice. Serves 4.

Suggested wine: Pinot Noir

Now State and local governments, along with private property owners, are implementing an extensive conservation plan of their own, which flies in the face of preservationism. They have developed a habitat conservation plan which views humans as part of the ecosystem. With the help of the Nature Conservancy, the area, twice the size of New Jersey containing 2.5 million people, including the cities of Austin and San Antonio, will continue to be habitat for humans and other species, where the economy and ecology can flourish together.

The plan, in a nutshell, calls for the preservation of the most essential tracts of land in the area, either publicly owned or bought from private landowners, as a total ecological system, without having to protect every scrap of habitat and every single species for miles around. In addition, an aquifer plan developed in Texas and endorsed by the Department of Interior, limits the pumpage in the Edwards Aquifer to 450,000 acre-feet of water per year, down from the normal 540,000 acre-feet per year. In this way, the economic viability of the communities can co-exist with preserving endangered species.

Some possible substitutions: Cheat Mountain salamander, Desert slender salamander, Red Hills salamander, San Marcos Salamander, Santa Cruz long-toed Salamander, Shenandoah salamander.

Oregon Silverspot Butterfly
Speyeria zerene hippolyta

Richard Schroeder planned most of his adult life to build a world-class golf course and resort on his parents property on the coast of Oregon. The acreage in Gearhart, Oregon was mostly cow pasture and open sage and dunes, with a lot of Scotch broom and a few common blue violets dotting the landscape. With his neighbors, and a financial backer, Schroeder spent ten years planning and designing his dream resort. Only to find out that the land was prime habitat for the Oregon silverspot butterfly.

Richard Schroeder worked diligently to accommodate the butterfly. He met with the silverspot recovery team made up of biologists and staffers of the USFWS. He hired an expert on the insect, Mr. Paul Hammond, of Oregon State University, to put together a conservation plan which called for using some habitat on the south end and planting habitat on the north end, but all was for naught. Hammond found an additional patch of butterfly habitat on the land, and while Fish and Wildlife Services picked the plan apart, Schroeder's financial backers pulled the plug in exasperation.

Society had chosen an insect over the dream of a human being, according to Schroeder, and how anyone is better off for it escapes logic.

As it turns out, Schroeder was not the only one in Clatsop County, Oregon, with a butterfly problem. Frank Hildreth and Donald Wudtke of Northwest Conference Resorts, tried to build another golf course and resort a few miles north of Gearhart. This, too, was silverspot butterfly habitat, but Hildreth and Wudtke were confident they could build around the silverspots, and bought 296 acres of grassy sand dunes.

Now, the silverspot butterfly is pretty picky when it comes to habitat. It seems the caterpillars only eat the common blue violet, so they lay their eggs near the violet exclusively. This is fine as long as there are common blue violets around, but left unattended, common blue violets become overrun by Scotch broom. In the old days, the Native Americans would periodically burn the scrub brush, and blue violets would flourish along with the butterflies. But since the 1930's when the US Forest Service started campaigning against fires, Scotch broom overwhelmed the six-inch violets, and with them the butterfly. More than nine-tenths of the habitat of the silverspot butterfly has disappeared through this natural evolution.

Hidreth and Wudtke have proposed setting aside twenty-five acres of their property as designated habitat to be managed for the silverspot butterfly, in return for permission to develop the rest of their property. At last word, USFWS was still sitting on their hands. However, without human intervention, the butterfly will surely go the way of its habitat, overrun by scrub, and all will lose.

Some other possible collectibles: Bay checkerspot butterfly, El Segundo blue butterfly, Kern primrose sphinx moth, Lange's metalmark butterfly, Lotis blue butterfly, Mission blue butterfly, Mitchell's satyr butterfly, Palos Verdes blue butterfly, San Bruno elfin butterfly, Schaus swallowtail butterfly, Smith's blue butterfly, Uncompahgre butterfly.

Maryland Darter
Etheostoma sellare

A cousin to the now famous snail darter in Tennessee, the Maryland darter is the nemesis of local farmers and ranchers. They have been required to halt the use of numerous pesticides on crops near Deer Creek, even though there has been no evidence that any pesticides have reached the creek.

Although this may seem like a local problem to many of us, the snail darter was able to stop the multi-million dollar Tellico Dam on the Little Tennessee River, even though it was half finished. It took an "act of Congress", literally, to complete the dam project, and after scientific research and widespread studies it was found that the snail darter flourished in many other populations, not counted when the species was listed as endangered.

PICKLED DARTER APPETIZER

10 one-half pound Maryland darter, filleted
1 teaspoon salt   1 cup water
1 cup white vinegar   1 large onion, sliced
$\frac{1}{2}$ cup sugar $1\frac{1}{2}$ T mixed pickling
Salad greens   spices
Sour cream   Dijon mustard

Day before, cut the darter fillets into two or three pieces and steam over boiling water on steamer for about seven minutes. Meanwhile, combine the salt, water, vinegar, onion, sugar and spices in a saucepan and bring to a boil. Place steamed darter in a ceramic bowl and pour hot pickling mixture over to cover. Cool. Chill overnight in the refrigerator.

Next day, drain darters. Serve on salad greens with sour cream flavored with mustard. Serves 8.

Suggested wine: Sauvignon Blanc

It is important to note that even if you don't live in Tennessee or Maryland, you can still have your darters of choice.

Some possible substitutions: Amber darter, Bayou darter, Boulder darter, Cherokee darter, Etowah darter, Fountain darter, Goldline darter, Leopard darter, Niangua darter, Okaloosa darter, Slackwater darter, Watercress darter, and other candidates waiting to be listed.

Fine-Rayed Pigtoe Pearly Mussel
Fusconaia cuneolus
Crackling Pearly Mussel
Hemistena lata

I have included these two fine specimens only because of the inordinate number of different species that have been listed on the Endangered Species list as threatened or endangered, and the list is growing. Currently, there are 52 different mussel species, sub-species or distinct populations listed as threatened or endangered throughout the United States. Tennessee, alone, has 28 of them, and Alabama is home to 26. There are an additional 10 mussels proposed to be listed on the Category 1 list and many others in the wings.

The majority of the mussels listed are freshwater mussels and have been affected by habitat reduction due to dams. However, it is glaringly apparent that the use of "distinct populations", in order to manipulate the total populations, played a critical part in the listing of most of these species.

Therefore, I have included the following scrumptious recipe.

PEARLY MUSSEL PASTA

Select mussels that are unbroken and tightly closed, or that close when pricked inside. Scrub mussels thoroughly, soak and debeard.

1 Tablespoon salt	1 Lb. dried spaghetti
$\frac{1}{2}$ dozen Fine-rayed pigtoe pearly	$\frac{1}{2}$ doz. Crackling
$\frac{1}{2}$ dozen Rough pigtoe pearly	pearly mussel
$\frac{1}{2}$ dozen Shiny pigtoe pearly	1 cup dry white wine
$\frac{2}{3}$ cup virgin olive oil	2 cloves garlic
1 teaspoon red pepper flakes	Fresh parsley

☞

Bring a large pot of water with 1 tablespoon of salt to a boil. Add the spaghetti and cook until firm but tender. While spaghetti is cooking, place the mussels in another large pot with the white wine and steam them until they open, approximately 3 to 5 minutes. Remove those that open to a bowl, and discard those that don't open. Shuck all but 2 of each type of mussel.

Heat the oil, minced garlic, and red pepper flakes over low heat in a saucepan. Just before pasta is done, remove the oil from the heat and add the shucked mussel meat.

Drain the pasta and toss with the hot oil and shucked mussel meat. Arrange the remaining unshucked mussels on top, sprinkle with chopped parsley, and serve. Serves 4.

Suggested wine: Sauvignon Blanc

Some Possible Substitutions: Alabama lamp pearly, Appalachian monkeyface pearly, Birdwing pearly, Cumberland bean pearly, Cumberland monkeyface pearly, Cumberland pigtoe, Curtis' pearly, Dromedary pearly, Fat pocket pearly, Green-blossom pearly, Higgins' eye pearly, Little-wing pearly, Orange-footed pearly, Pale Lilliput pearly, Pink mucket pearly, Purple cat's paw pearly, Tubercled-blossom pearly, Turgid-blossom pearly, White wartyback pearly, Yellow-blossom pearly, or any of the other 62+ mussels supposedly threatened.

Gray Wolf
Canis lupus

The gray wolf, recently re-introduced into Yellowstone National Park and central Idaho, has never been endangered from extinction, and is still plentiful throughout Canada and Alaska. As this country grew, and people made their way West, towns of farmers, ranchers, school teachers and store keepers sprouted up throughout the nation. In order to protect their livestock and their communities, a bounty was placed on wolves. Ranchers' efforts to eradicate the wolf was less than formidable, however, and in 1902, the Federal Government mounted an all-out campaign to kill wolves. In that year alone, according to Alston Chase's environmental classic "*Playing God in Yellowstone*", Government officials killed more than 1,800 wolves and 23,000 coyotes in 39 national forests.

In 1915, the Federal Government increased their assault, putting professional "wolfers" on the payroll of the National Biological Survey, known today as the US Fish and Wildlife Service. Furthermore, a directive in 1918 from the director of the Park Service to Yellowstone's acting superintendent ordered cooperation in the "extermination of wolves, coyotes, and mountain lions in Yellowstone National Park." A record 136 wolves were killed in Yellowstone that year.

SON-OF-A-GUN WOLF STEW

4 lb. wolf meat	1 bottle red wine
1 $10\frac{1}{2}$-oz can tomato soup	4 bay leaves
3 T Kitchen Bouquet	Parsley
Rosemary	6 stalks celery
6 onions, chopped	6 carrots, sliced
1 package frozen peas	

In a large kettle combine meat, soup, wine, and herbs. Cook for about $3\frac{1}{2}$ hours until meat is tender. Add the celery, onions and carrots and cook for $\frac{1}{2}$ hour more. Add the peas just before serving and cook only until they are tender. Serve with extra sourdough French bread.

Suggested wine: Gamay Beaujolais or hot brandy

    The movement to eradicate the wolf from populated areas, as well as national parks, was a rousing success by the 1940's. Since that time the populations of elk, white tail deer and pronghorn antelope have been on the increase. The population of elk in Yellowstone's northern herd alone numbers around 20,000. Sheep and cattle ranches have prospered without their main predators, and the national parks have enjoyed great success with visitors.

    With natural populations of wolves in Idaho, Montana, North Dakota and Minnesota ever increasing, why is it necessary to re-introduce this predator into other locations in the "lower 48"? Maybe it is because the FWS feels it needs to make amends for actions of an earlier agency, or maybe because of an outdated myth that "we have to go back to the way it was" in order to have a balance in nature.

STUFFED ALASKAN CABBAGE ROLLS

Boil one head Alaskan cabbage in water until soft. Drain and separate leaves on plate. In a deep Dutch oven, melt 1 tablespoon bacon fat. Mix following ingredients:

2 Lb. ground wolf meat	Salt and pepper
1 onion, chopped	1 t paprika
1 clove garlic, crushed	1 cup cooked rice

Place two large tablespoons of meat mixture on cabbage leaves. Fold the leaves around the meat securely. Place the cabbage rolls in the bacon fat. Simmer on low heat on top of stove. While the first layer of rolls are browning, add the following tomato mixture on the top:

1 can of large tomatoes	No. 2 can of
1 sm. can tomato sauce	sauerkraut (do not
2 Tablespoons sugar	use juice)

Continue to add a layer of cabbage rolls and a layer of tomato mixture until pot is full. Simmer with lid on for about 2 hours until done. Tastes better reheated slowly the next day. Serve with new potatoes and cucumber salad.

Suggested wine: Cabernet Sauvignon

Perhaps it is as Arlene Hanson, who lives near Cody, Wyoming and is head of the No Wolf Option Committee, believes. Bringing back the wolves, according to Hanson, is not about restoring the wilds, but about land, and who's in charge. "Once again", says Arlene, "the rugged rural folk who work the earth--and put food on other people's table--find their rights, their independence, indeed their very way of life, under assault by outside forces that care for them not a wit." It is the environmentalists, she says, who've found in the wolf the perfect proxy to further their own agenda. "The entire wolf issue is a land lockup issue," says Hanson. "It's a ploy by the environmentalists, the big, rich, monied organizations. They want more and more wilderness. They've found a new playground, and they want it all to themselves."

Prior to the introduction of the wolves, FWS collected comments from interested parties, which in hind site seem to have been disregarded. I think some of the more telling comments are worth repeating.

1) "Nobody has the right to endanger my life or my children's' lives by introducing predators that kill for a living."

2) "What we're afraid of is the land use restrictions that go along with the introduction of the wolf."

3) "My concern, as a state legislator, is that the wolf will be used to shut down industry, using the hammer of the Endangered Species Act."

4) "Wolves will simply lock up more land by the protection of corridors."

And from the other side of the spectrum, which relays our worst fears,

5) "Area's around wolf dens and congregating areas should be given seasonal closures to prevent disturbance...restrictions should be placed on use of roads, grazing, mining, and timbering."

And one of the best comments,

6) "There were wolves in the New York City area at one time. Why not plant a few there?"

Whether Arlene Hanson's beliefs will prove correct in the long run, time will tell. However, re-introduction of wolves certainly arms those who would use the Endangered Species Act to limit grazing and other multiple uses of our national forests and the private property bordering our national parks. Further pressure from animal rights activists would also hasten the halting of hunting elk and white tail deer in order to "feed the wolves." The Endangered Species Act is causing enough havoc with peoples' lives without reintroducing dangerous, carnivorous predators to areas where they were wiped out by the settlers years ago for the simple reason that they are dangerous, carnivorous predators.

WOLF CHOPS AND DRESSING

4 cups dry bread crumbs	$\frac{1}{4}$ t Bell's seasoning
3 T chopped onion	$\frac{1}{3}$ cup melted butter
1 teaspoon salt	Sage to taste
$\frac{1}{4}$ teaspoon pepper	Hot water to moisten

Toss dressing mix, above, gently to mix. Grease baking dish. Place 4 wolf chops in dish. Then add dressing mix, and place 4 more chops on top. Bake in oven one hour at 350° F. Serves 4.

Suggested wine: Merlot

Some possible substitutions: Eastern timber wolf, Mexican gray wolf, Northern Rocky Mountains gray wolf, Northern swift fox, Red wolf, San Joaquin kit fox, Santa Cruz fox.

CONCLUSION

In a letter to the US Fish and Wildlife Service in January 1995, Robert Thornton, in arguing against the re-listing of the California Gnatcatcher, summed up one of the most critical abuses of the Endangered Species Act by preservationists and environmental extremists. "The purpose of the ESA is to protect genetically unique life forms," Thornton states. "It does this by requiring that listings decisions be based on the 'best scientific . . . data available' and by requiring that a species or subspecies be threatened or endangered 'throughout all or a significant portion of its range.' The entire regulatory structure of the ESA becomes a sham if the taxonomy of a species or subspecies is manipulated to artificially restrict the range of the species. If the range of a 'species' can be arbitrarily restricted to qualify the species for listing (and thereby accomplish some perceived conservation objective), then virtually any species or subspecies will qualify for listing under the ESA."

This is exactly what caused the listing of the California Gnatcatcher, as well as the Northern Spotted Owl, not to save a species from extinction, but to blatantly halt all development and construction in Southern California, and to halt all logging in the Pacific Northwest. As currently written and interpreted by the courts, the ESA does not permit the FWS to consider economic or social impacts in determinations whether to list a species as endangered or threatened. It should not, therefore, be allowed to make those determinations based on incomplete, altered, or unsubstantiated "scientific data" presented by those with an ulterior motives and personal agendas.

It is necessary to put a higher burden of proof on environmentalists and scientists to provide data supporting a need to propose a species for listing. That proof must be sound scientific data above reproach, and subject to peer review.

Turning wild animals into pariahs certainly was not the intent of Congress or President Richard Nixon in 1973 when they created the act to protect species from extinction. However, the law's mandate to protect all species at any cost, imposing unwarranted restrictions on private land, has created just such a backlash. "By focusing the enormous power of the federal government on the supposed protection of rare species, the act has made rare species unwanted and has even encouraged some people to get rid of them," said Richard Stroup, a former Interior Department chief economist now with the Political Economy Research Center.

Cindy Domenigoni isn't taking any chances. They are now plowing all their land annually, regardless of whether they plant on it, for fear of providing habitat for the Stephens' kangaroo rat. This not only deviates from standard farm practices but leaves no native grassland at all.

"It's frustrating that you do something for many, many years that seems to be coexisting with species and the environment, and then they put a regulation on you. It's utterly crazy," Cindy Domenigoni said. "In a way, they are forcing people to go out and destroy habitat because of the way they are enforcing the law."

Ben Cone isn't taking any chances either. With red-cockaded woodpeckers on part of his land, Cone states, "I cannot afford to let those woodpeckers take over the rest of my property. I'm going to start massive clear-cutting. I'm going to a 40-year rotation instead of a 75 to 80-year rotation."

It is necessary to acknowledge, therefore, that private property rights are a mainstay for freedom and democracy. The ESA is making owners of private property renters on a federal estate, losing every meaningful incentive to care for the land. And since the majority of the public's wildlife depends upon privately owned habitat, the public should ante up. If the urban majority value wildlife as much as the polls tell us they do, then they should cease compelling the rural minority to provide habitat at their own peril and expense. The public has to compensate private landowners faced with burdensome regulations somehow.

As Chuck Cushman, who heads up the American Land Rights Association, said, "More species could be saved if habitat protection became voluntary and timber companies, farmers and others were willing partners with wildlife officials. We have tried a top down, police state, heavy-handed mentality which has destroyed the conservation ethic in this country. The other side has had 23 years to make their system work, and it hasn't worked."

The "other side" agrees. Sen. John H. Chafee, chairman of the environment committee and a strong proponent of the ESA, says we need reforms to streamline the process, promote innovative land-use agreements to resolve conflicts, stress ecosystems rather than single species and give incentives to property owners to conserve habitat rather than destroy it. Michael Bean, chairman of the Environmental Defense Fund's wildlife program and a co-author of the ESA, even agrees. "A legitimate problem is that the law does not explore the strategy of offering incentives to get [landowners] to do beneficial things for species," Bean states.

Requiring compensation of private property owners would make the government more innovative and reduce unwarranted restrictions on land. It would encourage voluntary efforts to protect the places where endangered species live, nest and feed. And compensation could be designed in many forms. Outright purchase of private property by the government or coalition of conservation groups, the purchase of development rights, cash "bounties" to landowners who allow populations of endangered species to reside on their property, and even free-market credits and tax incentives that can be accumulated and traded to other property owners, to name a few.

As R.J. Smith, senior environmental scholar at the Competitive Enterprise Institute, suggests, "Had the Endangered Species Act been in effect in 1900, countless wetland owners and volunteers might not have put up the nesting boxes that, along with closed seasons, were critical to the impressive recovery of the wood duck." Volunteerism works. Incentives work. Cost/risk analysis works. Heavy-handed regulations and land restrictions, as we have seen, do not work.

Rep. John Shadegg of Arizona agrees that the perverse incentives of the current law have to be reversed. "So long as the law says that the government can order you to do things and not do things that destroy the otherwise productive use of your land, we're going to have people who try to avoid the system," Shadegg says. "We want to create a structure that at least on private land, the motivation is to cooperatively work to protect those species."

The supporters of the Endangered Species Act are right: Protecting our natural heritage is a goal shared by the great majority of Americans. But the critics are right, too: The current law is unfair and unworkable. By imposing huge (though mostly hidden) costs on private landowners, the Endangered Species Act forces a luckless few to pay for environmental benefits enjoyed by everyone else.

Most people will agree, the act needs reform. Politicians, however, are understandably reluctant to propose the kind of bold reform the Endangered Species Act needs, given the opposition of the environmental establishment. After all, it is ostensibly "politically in-correct". But before Congress dismisses such far-ranging reforms it should consider this: Any attempt to modify the current law -- even piecemeal reform -- will raise the ire of the green lobby. Worse, when half-measures prove detrimental to both wildlife and property rights -- as they inevitably will -- Congress will have to wade into this morass again and again. Therefore, it behooves us all to get ESA reform right the first time.

SOURCES

"A Fairy Shrimp Tale", *The Wall Street Journal*, Editorial Article October 21, 1994.

"A Snail Retreat", *The Wall Street Journal*, Editorial Article December 27, 1993.

Adventures in Wine Cookery, California Winemakers, Edited by Bernice Glenn, Wine Advisory Board, 1965, San Francisco, CA.

American Game Cooking, John Ash and Sid Goldstein, Addison-Wesley Publishing Company, Inc., 1991, New York, NY.

Associated Press, "Fish Called Imperiled (But Is The Water, Too?)", *The New York Times*, March 6, 1993.

Associated Press, "Proposal To Ease Owl Policy", *The Press Democrat*, February 8, 1995.

Babbitt, Sect'y Bruce, "The Fierce Green Fire", *Audubon*, September-October 1994.

Balancing On The Brink Of Extinction, Edited by Kathryn A. Kohm, Island Press, 1991, Washington, DC.

Barbecuing, Grilling and Smoking, at the Academy, R. Clark, B. Aidells, C. Latimer, California Culinary Academy, Cole Group, 1994, Santa Rosa, CA.

Barro, Robert J., "Federal Protection -- Only Cute Critters Need Apply", *The Wall Street Journal*, August 4, 1994.

Baskin, Yvonne, "Trumpeter Swans Relearn Migration", *BioScience*, February 1993.

Baum, Bob, (AP), "Salmon Recovery Plan OK'd", *The Press Democrat*, December 15, 1994.

Baxley, Colette, (AP), "Woodpecker vs. Landowner: Who Will Foot The Bill?", Associated Press Release, January 31, 1994.

Beeton's Book of Household Management, Mrs. Isabella Beeton, S.O. Beeton, 1861, London, England. Reproduced by Jonathan Cape Limited, 1968.

Best, Robert K., "Species Habitat Rule is Less Caring for People", *In Perspective,* Spring 1995.

Brandon, Karen, "Texas Shrimp Farms Harvest a Jumbo Dilemma", *Los Angeles Times,* March 9, 1992.

Broken Trust Broken Land, Robert G. Lee, Book Partners, 1994, Wilsonville, Oregon.

Bryce, Robert, "Babbitt Backs Off on Bird", *The Christian Science Monitor,* September 30, 1994.

Building Supply Home Centers, Assoc. Publisher Patricia Coleman, A Cahners Publication, 1995, Des Plaines, IL.

Buzbee, Sally Streff, (AP), "State Issues Mountain Lion Warning", The Press Democrat", December 13, 1994.

Chadwick, Douglas H., "Dead or Alive, The Endangered Species Act", *National Geographic,* Vol. 187, No.3, March 1995, Washington, DC.

Clemings, Russell, (McClatchy News Service), "Farmer's Credibility On Trial In Rat Case", *The Press Democrat,* July 12, 1994.

Cone, Marla, "State Scientists Set Guidelines to Protect Bird", *Los Angeles Times,* April 1, 1993.

Cone, Marla, "Suit Claims US Fails to Protect Delta Smelt", *Los Angeles Times,* February 23, 1994.

Cone, Marla, "Clinton Proposes Reform of Law on Imperiled Species", *Los Angeles Times,* March 7, 1995.

Cone, Marla, "Endangered Species Act Is Now Looking to Save Itself", *Los Angeles Times,* June 26, 1995.

Conner, Doug, "Judge Rejects Challenges to Federal Logging Plan", *Los Angeles Times,* December 22, 1994.

Cooking Wild Game, Frank G. Ashrook and Edna N. Sater, Orange Judd Publishing Co., 1945, New York, NY.

"Cougar Attacks On the Increase In California", *The New York Times,* Editorial Article April 23, 1995.

Cushman, Chuck, "Law Deserves To Be Junked", *USA TODAY,* December 2, 1994.

Cushman, John H., Jr., "Eagles to Fly Free of the Endangered List", *The New York Times,* June 30, 1994.

De La Cruz, Donna, (AP), "Kill A Rat, Go To Jail? Man May Face Trial", *The Press Democrat,* August 11, 1994.

Diamond, John, (AP), "Woodpecker Stands Off 82nd Airborne", *The Press Democrat,* February 4, 1995.

Dinosaurs Walked Here, Patricia Lauber, Bradbury Press, 1987, New York, NY.

Diringer, Elliot, "Remaking the West: The Cody Saga", *San Francisco Chronicle*, December 13-14, 1994.

Dizerega, Gus, "True Endangered Species Reform", *The Press Democrat*, May 2, 1995.

Dominique's Famous Fish, Game and Meat Recipes, Dominique D'Ermo, Acropolis Books Ltd., 1981, Washington, DC.

"Don't Fire Up the Bulldozers Yet", *Los Angeles Times*, Editorial Article March 4, 1994.

Edible Plants and Animals; Unusual Foods from Aardvark to Zamia, A.D. Livingston and Helen Livingston, Facts on File, Inc., 1993, New York, NY.

"Endangered Species Survey Summary", California State Association of Counties, Agriculture & Natural Resources Committee, Supervisor Mary K. Shell, Chair, 1993.

Environmental Overkill, Whatever Happened to Common Sense?, Dixy Lee Ray with Lou Guzzo, Regnery Gateway, 1993, Washington, DC.

Essentials of Physical Anthropology, Nelson-Jurmain-Kilgore, West Publishing Co., 1992, St. Paul, MN.

Evergreen, Editor James D. Peterson, Evergreen Foundation, 1993, Medford, Oregon.

Everyday French Cooking, Henri-Paul Pellaprat, Rene Kramer, Publisher, 1968, Castagnola/Lugano, Switzerland.

Exotic Food, Rupert Croft-Cooke, George Allen and Unwin Ltd., 1969, London, England.

Facts About The States, Editor Joseph N. Kane, Steven Anzovin, Janet Podell, 2nd Edition, H.W. Wilson Co., 1993, New York, NY.

Fading Feast, Raymond Sokolov, Farrar-Straus-Giroux, 1979, New York, NY.

Fergus, Chuck, "The Florida Panther Verges on Extinction", *Science*, Vol 251, March 8, 1991.

Fitzgerald, Randy, "When a Law Goes Haywire", *Reader's Digest*, September 1993.

Food in History, Reay Tannahill, Crown Publishers, Inc., 1989, New York, NY.

Foster, David, (AP), "Land: Who's In The Right?", *The Press Democrat*, August 22, 1995.

Game Cookery in America and Europe, Raymond R. Camp, Coward-McCann, Inc., 1958, New York, NY.

Geniella, Mike, "Efforts to Protect Mountain Lions Have Worked -- All Too Well", *The Press Democrat*, August 17, 1994.

Geranios, Nicholas K., (AP), "2 More Mountain Lion Attacks", *The Press Democrat*, August 24, 1994.

"Good News For Gnats", *The Economist*, American Survey Article, September 7, 1991.

Grams, Rep. Rod, "Science, Not Politics" *GreenSpeak*, September 1994.

GreenSpeak, Editor Elizabeth Pease, National Hardwood Lumber Association, 1994, Memphis, TN.

Gugliotta, Guy, "Swan Song Becomes a Call to Action", *Washington Post*, May 18, 1993.

Gup, Ted, "Owl vs Man", Cover story *Time*, June 25, 1990.

Hanback, Michael, "Perilous Times for the Endangered Species Act", *Outdoor Life*, May 1994.

Harrington, Jim, "4-H Kids Targeted by Mail From Animal Rights Activists", McClatchy News Service, *The Press Democrat*, Aug. 12, 1994.

Herbert, H. Joseph, (AP), "Babbitt: No Endangered Property", *The Press Democrat*, August 12, 1994.

In Perspective, Robert K. Best, Pres., Pacific Legal Foundation, 1995, Sacramento, CA.

Jefferson, Jon, "Timmmberr!" and "Not-So-Sweet Home", *ABA Journal*, October 1993.

Johnson, Trevor and Helene Webb, "Attacks on Humans", *Los Angeles Times*, April 3, 1995.

"Judge Removes Protection From California Songbird", Special to *The New York Times*, May 4, 1994.

Kanamine, Linda, "Species Act Endangered? Support For Controversial Program Slips", *USA TODAY*, December 2, 1994.

Kay, Michele, (Cox News Service), "GOP Congress Likely to Slash Endangered Species Act Funds" *The Press Democrat*, Jan. 27, 1995.

Kenworthy, Tom, "Easing Protected Species Rules Intended to Gain Support" *The Washington Post*, March 7, 1995.

Knebel, John A., "Mining Law Change Reduces Tax Revenue", Letter to The *New York Times*, March 11, 1994.

Knickerbocker, Brad, "Federal Pact Aims to Avert Prospect of Spotted Owl II", *The Christian Science Monitor*, April 21, 1993.

Knickerbocker, Brad, "The Northwest's Showdown: Murrelets vs. Millworkers", *The Christian Science Monitor*, June 12, 1995.

Knickerbocker, Brad, "Endangered Species Act Weathers Court Battle", *The Christian Science Monitor*, June 30, 1995.

Kohlman, Matt, (AP), "Lawmakers Growl About Wolves", *The Press Democrat*, January 23, 1995.

"Lawsuits Promised Over Sea Turtle Deaths", Editorial Article, *Los Angeles Times*, June 7, 1994.

Legg, Robert F., "Woodpeckers, Owls, Rats, and Beetles", Temperate Forest
    Foundation, Beaverton, OR.
Living Things We Love To Hate, Des Kennedy, Whitecap Books, 1992,
    Vancouver, BC.
Log & Tally,   International Order of Hoo-Hoo Magazine,   Gurdon,
    Arkansas.
Mann, Charles C. and Mark L. Plummer, "The Butterfly Problem", *The
    Atlantic Monthly,* January 1992.
Mann, Charles C. and Mark L. Plummer, "The Noah Principle" *The New
    York Times,* May 11, 1992.
Mann, Charles and Mark L. Plummer, "The Geography of Endangerment",
    The Atlantic Monthly, December 1993.
Mann, Charles C. and Mark L. Plummer, "The High Cost of Biodiversity",
    Science, Vol. 260, June 25, 1993.
Mann, Charles C. and Mark L. Plummer, "Is Endangered Species Act in
    Danger?", *Science,* Vol. 267, March 3, 1995.
Mann, Charles C. and Mark L. Plummer, "Endangered Species Act: Finding
    a Better Balance", *The Christian Science Monitor,* July 31, 1995.
Mann, Charles C. and Mark L. Plummer, "California vs. Gnatcatcher",
    Audubon, January-February 1995.
Matthews, Jon, (McClatchy News), "Mountain Lions Called a Threat", *The
    Press Democrat,* March 28, 1995.
McCandless, Rep. Al and Rep. Jerry Lewis, "Blown Off by Environmental
    Extremists", Letter to *The Washington Post,* April 22, 1994.
McCoy, Charles, "U.S. Set to Unveil Plan in Bid to Save Songbird and Jobs",
    The Wall Street Journal, March 25, 1993.
McCoy, Charles, "Delta Smelt Is Placed On Endangered List By Wildlife
    Service", *The Wall Street Journal,* March 5, 1993.
McCoy, Charles, "Acreage Marked for Desert Tortoise Includes Disputed
    California Dump Site", *The Wall Street Journal,* February 9, 1994.
McCoy, Charles, "Citing Regulatory Errors, Judge Orders Songbird Off
    Endangered Species List", *The Wall Street Journal,* May 4, 1994.
McCoy, Charles, "Pacific Northwest Regulators Approve Plan to Cut Dam
    Power to Save Salmon", *The Wall Street Journal,* Dec. 15, 1994.
Modern Encyclopedia of Cooking, Vol. 1-2, Meta Given, J.G. Ferguson and
    Associates, 1947, Chicago, Illinois.
Moore, Patrick, "Hard Choices Ahead For Environmental Movement", *The
    Softwood Forest Products Buyer,* Nov/Dec 1994.
Murphy, Daniel J., "The GOP on Environmental Law", *Investor's Business
    Daily,* December 6, 1994.
Murphy, Dean E., "Fish's Threatened Status Raises Water Concerns", *Los
    Angeles Times,* March 5, 1993.

Murphy, Kim, "A Battle of Fish and Power Rages on Columbia River", *Los Angeles Times*, July 4, 1995.

Murphy, Kim, "Rewards For Saving Periled Species", *Los Angeles Times*, August 21, 1995.

National Geographic, "Rare Dwarf Mammoth Unearthed" and "First Look at a New Asian Mammal", January 1995.

National Wilderness Institute Resource, Director Robert E. Gordon, National Wilderness Institute, 1994, Washington, DC.

National Wildlife, Editor Mark Wexler, National Wildlife Federation, 1994, Vienna, VA.

Never Cry Wolf, Farley Mowat, Little, Brown, and Company, 1963, Boston, Massachusetts.

Noah, Timothy, "Fairy Shrimp Tale: Prawns in a Battle With Developers", *The Wall Street Journal*, March 10, 1994.

Out of Alaska's Kitchens, Alaska Crippled Children's Association, Inc., Rev. Ed., 1961, Anchorage, Alaska.

Pace, David, (AP), "Senators Propose Rewrite of Endangered Species Act", *The Press Democrat*, May 10, 1995.

Parrish, Michael, "Suit Filed to Ban Shrimp Imports That Endanger Sea Turtles", *Los Angeles Times*, February 25, 1992.

Parrish, Michael and Jesus Sanchez, "Flooded Farmers Blame State Policies on Wildlife", *Los Angeles Times*, March 17, 1995, pA1.

Pendleton, Scott, "US Pressures Shrimpers To Save Endangered Turtles", *The Christian Science Monitor*, August 2, 1994.

Peterson, James D., "Building Bridges of Understanding", *Evergreen*, Evergreen Foundation, Medford, OR.

Popiel, Leslie A., "Cost to Relocate Landfill Beetle Bugs Officials", *Christian Science Monitor*, Sept. 21, 1993.

Proctor, Owen, "Timber Issues Pose Challenge for Wood Exports/Imports", *Modern Woodworking*, October 1994.

Ratan, Suneel, "Socked By Sockeyes", *Fortune*, December 30, 1991.

Rattlesnake Under Glass, Martha Eastlake, Simon and Schuster, 1965, New York, NY.

Recipes: African Cooking, Time-Life Books, Time Inc., 1970, New York, NY.

Reiger, George, "Law of Nature", *Field and Stream*, March 1995.

Reinhold, Robert, "U.S. Acts To Save Home of Rare Bird", *The New York Times*, March 26, 1993.

Rice, James Owen, "Where Many An Owl Is Spotted", *National Review*, March 2, 1992.

Ridenour, David A., "To Save Wildlife, Scrap the Endangered Species Act", *The Wall Street Journal*, July 18, 1995.

Robertson, Lance, "Beyond the Rhetoric; Fact, Fiction and the Endangered Species Act, *The Press Democrat*, May 28, 1995.

Royko, Mike, "Animal Rights Tales are a Hoot and Howl", *Chicago Tribune*, August 14, 1995.

Rudner, Ruth, "Tracking in Yellowstone, Just Ahead of the Wolves", *The Wall Street Journal*, October 6, 1994.

Savage, David G., "Property Rights Bill Advances", *Los Angeles Times*, February 17, 1995.

Schneider, Kieth, "One Word May Decide Ruling on Owl, Land Rights", *The New York Times*, Jan. 6, 1995.

Schumacher, Rich, "The Temperate Forest Foundation", *Log and Tally*, August 1994.

Shelter, Editor Joyce Powell, Associations Publications, Inc., 1995, Collierville, TN.

Skelton, George, "Roundabout Fix To The Broken Delta", *Los Angeles Times*, April 1, 1993.

Soul Food, Jim Harwood and Ed Callahan, Nitty Gritty Productions, 1969, San Francisco, CA.

Southern Lumberman, Editor Nanci P. Gregg, Greysmith Publishing, Inc., 1995, Franklin, TN.

Stevens, William K., "Novel Strategy Puts People At Heart Of Texas Preserve", *The New York Times*, March 31, 1992.

Sugg, Ike, "Ecosystem Babbitt-Babble", *Wall Street Journal*, April 2, 1993.

Sugg, Ike, "Endangered Ecosystems: Babbitt's Ecobabble", *National Review*, September 20, 1993.

Sugg, Ike, "California Fires -- Losing Houses, Saving Rats", *The Wall Street Journal*, November 10, 1993.

Sugg, Ike, "Worried About That Owl On Your Land? Here's Good News", *The Wall Street Journal*, April 6, 1994.

Sugg, Ike, "Let's Don't Endanger the Truth", Letter to *The Wall Street Journal*, May 31, 1994.

Sugg, Ike, "A New Mythology Grows Up Around Wolves", Letter to *The New York Times*, June 30, 1994.

"Swan Song For Gnatcatcher?", *Christian Science Monitor*, Editorial Article May 6, 1994.

Sweeney, Frank, "Huge Water Project to Protect a Bird, Mouse", *Knight-Ridder Tribune*, January 6, 1995.

Sweeney, James, "Environment Battle on the Brink of War", *The Press Democrat*, April 25, 1995.

Seely, Eric S., "Endangered Species Insanity Must Stop", *The Press Democrat*, April 26, 1995.

Tainted Truth, The Manipulation of Fact in America, Cynthia Crossen, Simon and Schuster, 1994, New York, NY.

Taylor, Jeff A., "Turning Back The Green Wave?", *Investor's Business Daily,* September 19, 1995.

Taylor, Rob, "Judge OKs Northwest Forest Plan", *Post-Intelligencer,* December 22, 1994.

The Butterflies of North America, William H. Howe, Doubleday & Co., 1975, Garden City, NY.

The Cave Bear Story, Bjorn Kurten, Columbia University Press, 1976, New York, NY.

"The Emotional Species Act", *The Wall Street Journal,* Editorial Article Nov. 2, 1993.

"The Endangered Gremlins Act", *The Wall Street Journal,* Editorial Article June 3, 1994.

"The Endangered 100", *Life,* Editor-In-Chief Jason McManus, Time Inc., September 1994.

The Fish Book, a Seafood Menu Cookbook, Kelly McCune, Harper and Row, 1988, New York, NY.

The Frugal Gourmet Cooks Three Ancient Cuisines, Jeff Smith, William Morrow and Company, Inc., 1989, New York, NY.

The Lily Wallace New American Cook Book, Lily Haxworth Wallace, Books, Inc., 1944, New York, NY.

The Merchant Magazine, Editor/Publisher David Cutler, The Merchant Magazine, Inc., 1995, Newport Beach, CA.

The New York Times Heritage Cook Book, Jean Hewitt, Bonanza Books, 1972, New York, NY.

The Official World Wildlife Fund Guide to Endangered Species of North America, Vol. 1-4, Beacham Publishing, 1992, Washington, DC.

These Are The Endangered, Charles Cadieux and Bob Hines, The Stone Wall Press, Inc., 1981, Washington, DC.

The Wild Palate, Walter and Nancy Hall, Rodale Press, 1980, Emmaus, Pennsylvania.

Turque, Bill, "The West", and "Nature at Risk: A Reader's Guide", *Newsweek,* September 30, 1991.

Tyson, James L., "Tilling Middle Ground of Property-Rights Debate", *The Christian Science Monitor,* June 27, 1995.

US Fish and Wildlife Service, "Formal Consultation on Farmers Home Administration (FmHA) Loan Program, April 26, 1993.

Western Civilization, Vol. 1, Jackson J. Spielvogel, West Publishing Co., 1991, St. Paul, MN.

Why Did The Dinosaurs Disappear?, Dr. Phillip Whitfield, Viking Press, 1991, New York, NY.

Widman's World Wood Review, Editor Charles R. Widman, 1994, Vancouver, BC.

"Wolves Leave Pens at Yellowstone and Appear to Celebrate", *The New York Times, National Report,* March 27, 1995.

Wood, Daniel B., "Babbitt Endorses Texas Aquifer Plan", *Christian Science Monitor,* April 21, 1993.

Wood Technology, Editor David Pease, Miller Freeman, Inc., 1994, San Francisco, CA.

Woman's Day Encyclopedia of Cookery, Vol. 4, Ed. Eileen Tighe, Fawcett Publications, Inc., 1966, New York, NY.

Young, Tobias, "Conflict Rises With Cougar Population", *The Press Democrat,* May 23, 1995.

Zausner, Steven, "Learning From Mistakes", Forbes, April 12, 1993.

INDEX

A

Age of Dinosaurs, 1
Alabama Beach Mouse, 129
Alabama Cavefish, 19
Alabama Cave Shrimp, 78
Alabama Lamp Pearly, 139
Alabama Red-Bellied Turtle, 95
Alamosa Springsnail, 57
Alaska, 9,24,64,139
Alexander, Charles, 29
Aleutian Canada Goose, 68
Amargosa Vole, 53
Amber Darter, 137
American Bat Conservation
        Society, 96
American Burying Beetle, 64
American Land Rights Assoc,147
American Pergrine Falcon, 68
Ammonites, 1
Anastasia Island Beach Mouse,
        129
Anderson and Middleton, 124
Apache Trout, 100
Appalachian Monkeyface Pearly
        Mussel, 139
Arroyo, Darron, 73
Arthur, William, 31

Artic Fox, 3
Artic Perigrine Falcon, 68
Ash Meadows Speckled Dace,131
Atlantic Green Turtle, 17,18,95
Atlantic Monthly, 13
Atlantic Tuna Fishing, 6
Attwater's Greater Prairie
        Chicken, 125
Atwood, Dr. Jonathan, 107-108
Australian Mulberry, 41

B

Babbitt, Interior Sect'y Bruce,
        24,39,47,84,102,106,125
Babbitt v Sweethome, 32,121
Bachman's Wood Warbler, 103
Bald Eagle, 8-9,18,19,64-68
Bannister, Richard, 58
Barbate June Beetle, 62-64
Barone, John, 110
Barro, Robert J., 19
Bay Checkerspot Butterfly, 135
Bayou Darter, 135
Bean, Michael, 147
Beaver, 3
Big Horn Sheep, 3
Big Spring Spinedace, 131
Birdwing Pearly Mussel, 139
Bison, 3
Bittman, Roxanne, 76
Black Bear, 3,106
Black-Capped Vireo, 18,87-88,
        101,103,111
Blackside Dace, 131
Blue Shiner, 131
Blue-Tailed Mole Skink, 91
Blunt-Nosed Leopard
        Lizard, 17,89-91
Bone Cave Harvestmen, 103
Bonytail Chub, 18,55,98
Borax Lake Chub, 100
Boreal Owl, 125

Boulder Darter, 137
Bridled White-Eye, 89
Brooks, David, 29
Brown-Headed Cowbird, 88
Brown Pelican, 68
Bruneau Hot Springsnail, 56-57
"Buffalo Commons", 24
Bureau of Land Management, 91
Bynum, Henry, 82

C

Cahuilla tribe, 51
California Clapper Rail, 125-129
California Condor, 68
*California Desert Protection
        Act*, 92
California Freshwater Shrimp, 78
California Gnatcatcher, 87, 106-
        111,145
California Least Tern, 89
Cameroon vine, 42
Cape Fear Shiner, 131
Cape Sable Seaside Sparrow, 113
Carolina Northern Flying
        Squirrel, 75
Casper's Regional Park, 73
Cave Crayfish, 78
Center for Disease Control, 96
Chafee, Sen. John, 147
Channel Islands, 3
Chase, Alston, 140
Cheat Mountain Salamander, 133
Cherokee Darter, 137
Chihuahua Chub, 100
Child, Brandt and Venice, 53-56
Chimney Cave Shrimp, 78
Chinook Salmon, 100
Chittenango Ovate Ambersnail,57
Choctawahatchee Beach
        Mouse, 19,129
Christy, Richard P., 104
Christy v Hodel, 104

Cleveland National Forest, 51
Clinton, President Bill, 68,102
Clinton, Hillary, 67
Clover Valley Speckeled
        Dace, 131
Coachella Valley Fringe-Toed
        Lizard, 91
Cockburn, Alexander, 31
Coffin Cave Mold Beetle, 64
Coho Salmon, 100
Colorado Squawfish, 18,55,98-99
Competitive Enterprise
        Institute, 81,148
Conasauga Logperch, 131
Cone, Benjamin, 80,146
Conservancy Fairy Shrimp, 76
Crackling Pearly Mussel, 138
Crested Honeycreeper, 115
Cumberland Bean Pearly Mussel,
        139
Cumberland Monkeyface Pearly
        Mussel, 139
Cumberland Pigtoe Mussel, 139
Curtis' Pearly Mussel, 139
Cushman, Chuck, 147
Cuyamaca Rancho State Park, 73

D

Davis, Maj. Gen. Richard, 85
DDT, 8,9,64
Death Valley Nat'l Monument, 92
Delemnites, 1
Delhi Sands Flower-Loving
        Fly, 86
Del Mar Manzanita, 110
Delmarva Peninsula Fox
        Squirrel, 75
Delta Green Ground Beetle, 64
Delta Smelt, 129-131
Desert Dace, 131
Desert Slender Salamander, 133
Desert Tortoise, 30,91-95

Desert Tortoise Mgt. Zone, 95
Dinosaurs, 1
Distinct Population, 12-13,138
Domenigoni family, 49,146
Dromedary Pearly Mussel, 139
Dusky Seaside Sparrow, 113
Dwarf Mammoth, 3

E

East Mojave Nat'l Scenic Area, 92
*Eastern Pacific Tuna
        Fishing*, 6
Eastern Cougar, 73
Eastern Timber Wolf, 144
Edwards Aquifer, 131
Ehrenfeld, David, 10
Eisner, Tom, 42
Elk, 3,141,143
El Segundo Blue Butterfly, 135
Erlich, Paul, 30
Ergot, 41
Ermine, 3
Etowah Darter, 137
Evans, Brock, 31-32
Everglades Nat'l Park, 69
Everglade Snail Kite, 115

F

Fat Pocket Pearly Mussel, 139
Fike, Scott, 71
Fine-Rayed Pigtoe Pearly
        Mussel, 138-139
*Fish and Seafood
        Promotion Act*, 6
Fish and Wildlife Ser., 7,8,9,13,
        14,15,16,17,18,20,21,22,
        23,29,30,40,46,49,51,54,
        55,56,57,63,69,70,73,74,
        76,79,84,86,89,91,98100
        102,103,107,108,110115
        118,124,125,127,131134
        135,140,145

*Fishery Conservation
        and Mgt Act*, 6
Fitzgerald, Randy, 43
Fitzpatrick, Lesley, 74
Flat-Spired Snail, 57
Flattened Musk Turtle, 95
Florida Panther, 19,69-73
Florida Panther Nat'l Wildlife
        Refuge, 69
Florida scrubjay, 17,18,19,87,
        113-115
FmHA, 56
Foote, Devon, 73
Foreman, Dave, 22
Forest Conservation
        Council, 23
Forest Service, US, 83,120
Fort Bragg, NC, 85
Foskett Speckled Dace, 131
Fountain Darter, 137
Framton, George, 93
Fresno Flood Control Dist, 115
Fresno Kangaroo Rat, 12,53
Friedman, Milton, 22

G

*Game and Bird
        Preserves...Act*, 6
Garcia, Yshmael, 46
Gaviota State Park, 73
Georgia-Pacific, 84
Giant Kangaroo Rat, 12,53
Gila Trout, 100
Golden-Cheeked Warbler, 100-
        103,111
Goldline Darter, 137
Gopher Tortoise, 95
Gomez, Lucy, 72
Graham, Robert, 40-41
Grasshopper Sparrow, 111-113
Gray Bat, 96-97
Gray Whale, 9

Gray Wolf, 139-144
Greenback Cutthroat Trout, 100
Green-Blossom Pearly Mussel,
          139
Green Sea Turtle, 95
Grizzly Bear, 3,9,19,104-106
Guam Rail, 129
Guifoyle, Joan, 8

H

Habitat Conservation Plans, 124
Hall, Stephen, 130
Hammond, Paul, 134
Hanson, Arlene, 142
Hatfield, Sen. Mark, 7
Hawaiian Common Moorhen, 125
Hawaiian Crow, 85
Hawaiian Dark-Rumped Petrel, 85
Hawaiian Duck, 68
Hawaiian Goose, 68
Hawaiian Hawk, 68
Hawaiian Hoary Bat, 97
Hawksbill Sea Turtle, 95
Hermann Kangaroo Rat, 12
Higgins' Eye Pearly Mussel, 139
Hildreth, Frank, 134
Hot Creek, 56
Hualapai Mexican Vole, 53
Humane Society, 91,95
Humpback Chub, 18,98
Hughes, Heidi, 96
Hungerford's Crawling Water
          Beetle, 64
Hunt, Jeanie, 55
Hutton Tui Chub, 100
Hyde, Dayton, 65

I

Independence Valley Speckeled
          Dace, 131
Indiana Bat, 97
Iowa Pleistocene Snail, 2,57

Island Night Lizard, 91
Ivory Billed Woodpecker, 85

J

Jaguarundi, 73
Jefferson, Thomas, 30
*Jellyfish or Sea Nettles.
          ..etc Act*, 6
Joshua Tree Nat'l Park, 92

K

Kanab Amber Snail, 53-56
Kemp's Ridley Sea Turtle, 95
Kendall Warm Springs Dace, 131
Kenna, Iris, 71
Kentucky Cave Shrimp, 78
Kern Primrose Sphinx Moth, 135
Key Largo Cotton Mouse, 129
Key Largo Woodrat, 53
Kirtland's Warbler, 103
Klimko, Anna, 46
Kowalski, Lisa, 73
Kretschmarr Cave Mold
          Beetle, 64,103
Krueger, Roger and Marj, 100
Kurten, Bjorn, 2

L

Lahontan Cutthroat Trout, 100
Lange's Metalmark Butterfly, 135
Large Kauai Thrush, 115
Laysan Duck, 68
Laysan Finch, 89
Least Bell's Vireo, 19,89
Least Tern, 89
Leatherback Sea Turtle, 95
Legg, Robert, 10
Leopard Darter, 137
Liddy, G. Gordon, 49
Light-Footed Clapper Rail, 129
Little Kern Golden Trout, 100

Little Mariana Fruit Bat, 97
Little-Wing Pearly Mussel, 139
Loggerhead Turtle, 17,95
Longhorn Fairy Shrimp, 76
Los Angeles Water Dept., 51
Los Padres Nat'l Forest, 73
Lotis Blue Butterfly, 135
Louisiana Black Bear, 106
Lovejoy, Thomas, 45

M

MacKinnon, John, 4
Mammoths, 3
Manitoba Toad, 80
Mann, Charles C., 13
Mann, Michael, 36
Marbled Murrelet, 85,124
Margay, 73
Mariana Common Moorhen, 125
Mariana Crow, 85
Mariana Fruit Bat, 97
Mariana Mallard, 68
*Marine Mammals
        Protection Act*, 6,9
Marine Sanctuaries, 6
Marx, Groucho, 11
Maryland Darter, 135
Masked Bobwhite, 115
Maui Parrotbill, 85
Melbane, Mark, 115
Mellon, Justin, 73
Merriam's Kangaroo Rat,12,53
Metrick, Andrew, 18,19
Mexican Gray Wolf, 144
Mexican Long-Nosed Bat, 97
Mexican Spotted Owl, 116,
        119,125
Ming-Lin, Taung, 52
Mission Blue Butterfly, 135
Mitchell's Satyr Butterfly, 135
Moapa Dace, 131
Mojave Tui Chub, 100

Molokai Thrush, 115
Mona Ground Iguana, 91
Monito Gecko, 19,91
Moore, Patrick, 26-28
Moose, 3
Morian, Beth, 87
Morro Bay Kangaroo Rat, 53
Mount Graham Red
        Squirrel, 73-75
Mountain Goat, 3
Mowat, Farley, 52
Moyers, George, 36
Mule Deer, 3
Murray Pacific Corp, 124
Murray, Toby, 124
Musk Oxen, 3

N

Nashville Crayfish, 78
National Audobon Soc., 27,31,37,
        118
*Nat'l Fish and Wildlife
        Foundation*, 6
Nat'l Forests Act, 6
National Geographic, 3,4
Nat'l Marine Fisheries
        Service, 16,17,20,23
Nat'l Park Service, 20,92
Nat'l Park Service Act, 5
National Resources/Envir, 15
National Wilderness
        Institute, 8,17,18,20,58
Natural Communities
        Conservation Plan, 106
Natural Resources Defense
        Council, 107
Nature Conservancy, 27,42,89,
        133
Nelson's Antelope Ground
        Squirrel, 75
Newsweek, 30,116
New York Times, The, 8

Niangua Darter, 137
Nightingale Reed Warbler, 103
Nihoa Finch, 89
Nixon, Richard M., 7,146
Noah Principle, The, 10,11
Noonday Snail, 57
Northeastern Beach Tiger
            Beetle, 59,64
Northern Aplomado Falcon, 68
Northern Rocky Mountain Gray
            Wolf, 144
Northern Swift Fox, 144
Northwest Conference Resorts,
            134
*North Pacific Halibut
            Fishing Act*, 6
Noss, Reed F., 22

O

Oahu Tree Snail, 57
Ocelot, 73
Off, Ted, 89
Okaloosa Darter, 137
Olive Ridley Sea Turtle, 95
Operation Stronghold, 65
Orange-Footed Pearly Mussel,139
Oregon Silverspot Butterfly,
            133-135
Orem, Betty, 120
O'Toole, Randall, 30,116
Otter, 3
Owens Tui Chub, 100
Ozark Big-Earred Bat, 95

P

Pacific Legal Fdn, 21
*Pacific Salmon Fishing
            Act, 6*
Pacific Yew Tree, 41
Pahranagat Roundtail Chub, 100
Painted Snake Coiled Forest
            Snail, 57

Paiute Cutthroat Trout, 100
Pale Lilliput Pearly Mussel, 139
Palos Verdes Blue Butterfly, 135
Pecos Bluntnose Shiner, 131
Pendley, William Perry, 24
Perdido Key Beach Mouse, 129
Peregrine Falcon, 9,19,68
Pinehurst Resort, 39
Pink Mucket Pearly Mussel, 139
Piping Plover, 89,113
Pixley Nat'l Wildlife Refuge, 89
Playing God In Yellowstone, 140
Plesiosaurs, 1
Plummer, Mark L., 13
Plymouth Red-Bellied Turtle, 95
Polar Bear, 3
Political Economy Research
            Center, 146
Ponape Mountain Starling, 113
*Protection and Conser.
            of Wildlife Act*, 6
*Protection of Migratory
            Game...Act*, 6
*Protection of Fur Seals..
            .. Act*, 6
Pterosaurs, 1
Puerto Rico Parrot, 85
Puerto Rico Plain Pigeon, 85
Puma, 73
Puritan Tiger Beetle, 58-59
Purple Cat's Paw Pearly Mussel,
            139
Purple Foxglove, 41

Q

R

Rains, Michael T., 24
Rapoport, Mark S., 96
Ray, Dixie Lee, 14,22,28,43
Razorback Sucker, 18,98

Reader's Digest, 43
RECIPES,
  Baked Mealies and
    Tomatoes, 63
  Baked Squawfish w/
    Caper Butter, 99
  Black-Capped Vireo
    Purleau, 87
  Blunt-Nosed Leopard
    Lizard Matelote, 90
  Chinese Smoked Spotted
    Owl, 121
  Conservancy Fairy
    Shrimp Canapés, 76
  Cooper's Entrecote, 48
  Delta Smelt Antipasti,
    129
  Desert Tortoise Prep-
    eration, 92
  Desert Tortoise Soup, 94
  Elderberry Wine, 60
  Farley's Creamed Tipton
    K-Rat, 52
  Fillets of Chub Orly, 100
  French-Fried Wyoming
    Toad Legs, 79
  Fricassee of Spotted Owl
    Roman Style, 117
  Golden-Cheeked Warb-
    ler on Toast, 102
  Grasshopper Sparrow
    pie, 113
  Grizzly Bear Loin
    Steaks, 105
  Hyde's Wild Eagle with
    Sauerkraut, 66
  Italian Gnatcatcher, 109
  Longhorn Fairy Shrimp
    in Tomato Aspic, 77
  Marinated Grilled Scrub
    Jays, 114

Mountain Lion Meat-
  loaf, 71
Mt. Graham Red
  Squirrel Brunswick
  Stew, 75
Panther Cutlet Forester
  Style, 70
Pearly Mussel Pasta, 138
Pickled Darter
  Appetizer, 137
Potted Bat Eastlake, 97
Puritan Tiger Beetles &
  Other Coleoptera, 58
Red-Cockaded Wood-
  pecker Sour Cream
  Fricassee, 83
Red-Cockaded Wood-
  pecker Spagetti, 84
Rasberry Glazed Spotted
  Owl, 120
Roast Gnatcatcher, 107
Roast Kangaroo Rat a la
  Riverside, 47
Roast Owl Breast in
  Orange Sauce, 123
Roast Red-Cockaded
  Woodpecker w/
  Chives, 81
Salt Marsh Harvest
  Mouse Stew, 126
Smothered California
  Clapper Rail, 128
Snake River Salmon
  Bait, 57
Son-Of-A-Gun Stew, 140
Stephen's Kangaroo Rat
  Taco, 50
Stuffed Alaskan Cabbage
  Rolls, 142
Stuffed Kanab Amber-
  snails, 55

Stuffed Spotted Owl, 118
Sweet and Sour Panther
    Roast, 72
Texas Blind Salamander
    Shish Kebab, 132
Toasted Elderberry
    Longhorn Beetle, 62
Tortoise a la King, 95
Vernal Pool Fairy
    Shrimp Cocktail
        Sauce, 78
Wolf Chops and
    Dressing, 144
Red-Cockaded Woodpecker, 19,
    30,34,40,80-85
Red Fox, 3
Red Hills Salamander, 19,133
Red Wolf, 144
*Regulation of Whaling
    Act*, 6
Reilly, William, 33
Rice Rat, 53
Richards, Gov. Ann, 102
Riendeer, 3
Riggs, Alan and Bonny, 68
Ringed Sawback Turtle, 95
Riverside Habitat Conservation
    Agency, 49
Roseate Tern, 89
Rosy Periwinkle, 41
Roush, Jon, 31
Rowe, Michael, 48
Ryan, Judge Harold, 57

S

"Safe Harbor", 39
Sanborn's Long-Nosed Bat, 97
San Bruno Elfin Butterfly, 135
San Clemente Sage Sparrow, 113
Sand Skink, 19,91
San Joaquin Kit Fox, 144
San Marcos Salamander, 131-133

Santa Cruz Fox, 12,144
Santa Cruz Long-Toed
    Salamander, 133
*Salmon and Steelhead
    Conservation..*, 6
Salt Marsh Harvest Mouse,
    125-129
Sao La, 4
Scalia, Justice Antonin, 33
Schneider, Stephen, 28
Schoener, Barbara, 72
Schroeder, Richard, 133-134
Science, 13
Schaus Swallowtail Butterfly,
    17,135
Shadegg, Rep. John, 148
Shasta Crayfish, 78
Shenandoah Salamander, 133
Sher, Vic, 37
Shorelands Company, 125,127
Shuler, John, 105
Sierra Club, 31,37,131
Sierra Club Legal Defense
    Fund, 30,37,116
Simpson Timber Co, 124
Slackwater Darter, 137
Slender Chub, 100
Small Kauai Thrush, 115
Small, Laura, 73
Smathers, Webb, 83
Smith, R.J., 81,148
Smith's Blue Butterfly, 135
Snake River Sockeye Salmon, 100
Snowshoe Hare, 3
Snowy Plover, 113
Socorro Springsnail, 57
Sonora Chub, 100
Southern Beach Mouse, 129
*South Pacific Tuna
    Fishing*, 6
Sporkin, Judge Stanley, 108
Spotfin Chub, 100

Spotted Owl, 11,14,18,19,23,29
       30,33,34,116-125,145
Stahl, Andy, 116
St. Croix Ground Lizard, 91
Steiner, Gen. Carl, 85
Stephen's Kangaroo Rat, 12,46-51
Stewart, Dwight, 83
Stroup, Richard, 146
Swainson's Hawk, 68
Swamp Pink, 18
Sweethome v Babbitt, 121
Sweitzer, Judge Harvey, 29
Symington, Gov. Fife, 25

T

Tauzin/Hansen Amendment, 93
Tallico Dam, 136
Temperate Forest
       Foundation, 10
Texas Blind Salamander, 19,34,
       131-132
Thoreau, Henry David, 49
Thornton, Robert, 145
Timber Wolves, 3,139-144
Time, 29
Tipton Kangaroo Rat, 12,51-53
Title 16, 5
Tooth Cave Ground Beetle,64,103
Tooth Cave Pseudoscorpions, 103
Tooth Cave Spider, 103
Trotter, David, 103
True, Todd, 37
Tubercled-Blossom Pearly, 139
Tulare Pseudobahia Plant, 115
Turgid-Blossom Pearly, 139
Tule Vista Farms, 89
Tulotoma Snail, 57
Twain, Mark, 29

U

Uncompahgre Butterfly, 135

UN Conference on Environ.
       & Development, 25
Utah Valvata Snail, 57

V

Valley Elderberry Longhorn
       Beetle, 59-62
Vernal Pool Fairy Shrimp, 76
Virginia Big-Earred Bat, 97
Virginia Northern Flying
       Squirrel, 75
Virgin River Chub, 100

W

Waccamaw Silverside, 19
Walker Jr., Donald, 23
Wall Street Journal, The, 23,29,
       42,96,101
Ward Valley, 92
Washington Post, The, 7
Watercress Darter, 137
Weitzman, Martin, 18,19
West Indian Manatee, 19
Westvaco Corp, 40,84
*Whale Conservation and
       Protection...*, 6
White, Justice Byron, 104
White-Necked Crow, 85
White Wartybacked Pearly, 139
Whitfield, Dr. Phillip, 2
Whooping Crane, 9,19
Wiedenmann, Kurt, 37
Wilderness Society, 9,31
*Wild Horses and Burros..
       ..Act*, 7
Wildlands Project, 22
Wilson, E.O., 11,58
Wolly Mammoths, 3
Wood Stork, 85
Wood Warbler, 103
World Wildlife Fund, 3,27,45
Wudtke, Donald, 134

Wyoming toad, 2,79-80

Y
Yaqui Catfish, 100
Yaqui Chub, 100
Yellow-Blossom Pearly, 139
Yellow-Blotched Map Turtle, 95
Yellow Shouldered Blackbird,115
Yellowstone Nat'l Prk, 5,139,140,
        141
Yosemite Nat'l Park, 5
Yuma Clapper Rail, 129

SEND A COPY TO YOUR CONGRESSMAN

104th Congress
United States House of Representatives

Mail is addressed to the building --

- Room number with three digits, Cannon Building
- Room number with four digits starting with 1, Longworth Bldg.
- Room number with four digits starting with 2, Rayburn Building

Mail to your Representative, Bldg Name, Rm No., Washington, DC 20515.

Representatives

Name	Room
Abercrombie, Neil (D) HI	1233
Ackerman, Gary (D) NY	2243
Allard, Wayne (R) CO	422
Andrews, Robert (D) NJ	2439
Archer, Bill (R) TX	1236
Armey, Richard (R) TX	301
Bachus, Spencer (R) AL	127
Baesler, Scotty (D) KY	113
Baker, Richard (R) LA	434
Baker, William (R) CA	1724
Baldacci, John (D) ME	1740
Ballenger, Cass (R) NC	2238
Barcia, James (D) MI	1410
Barr, Bob (R) GA	1607
Barrett, Bill (R) NE	1213
Barrett, Bobby (D) WI	1224
Bartlett, Roscoe (R) MD	322
Barton, Joe (R) TX	2264
Bass, Charles (R) NH	1728
Bateman, Herbert (R) VA	2350
Becerra, Xavier (D) CA	1119
Beilenson, A. (D) CA	2465
Bentsen, Ken (D) TX	128
Bereuter, Doug (R) NE	2348
Berman, Howard (D) CA	2231
Bevill, Tom (D) AL	2302
Bilbray, Brian (R) CA	1004
Bilirakis, Michael (R) FL	2240
Bishop, Sanford (D) GA	1632
Bliley, Thomas (R) VA	2241
Blute, Peter (R) MA	1029
Boehlert, Sherwood (R) NY	2246
Boehner, John (R) OH	1011
Bonilla, Henry (R) TX	1427
Bonior, David (D) MI	2207
Bono, Sonny (R) CA	512
Borski, Robert (D) PA	2182
Boucher, Fred (D) VA	2245

Name	Room
Brewster, Bill (D) OK	1727
Browder, Glen (D) AL	2344
Brown, Corrine (D) FL	1610
Brown, George (D) CA	2300
Brown, Sherrod (D) OH	1019
Brownback, Sam (R) KS	1313
Bryant, Ed (R) TN	1516
Bryant, John (D) TX	2330
Bunn, Jim (R) OR	1517
Bunning, Jim (R) KY	2437
Burr, Richard (R) NC	1431
Burton, Dan (R) IN	2411
Buyer, Stephan (R) IN	326
Callahan, Sonny (R) AL	2418
Calvert, Ken (R) CA	1034
Camp, Dave (R) MI	137
Canady, Charles (R) FL	1222
Cardin, Ben (D) MD	104
Castle, Michael (R) DE	1207
Chabot, Steve (R) OH	1641
Chambliss, Sandy (R) GA	1708
Chapman, Jim (D) TX	2417
Chenoweth, Helen (R) ID	1722
Christensen, Jon (R) NE	1020
Chrysler, Dick (R) MI	327
Clay Bill (D) MO	2306
Clayton, Eva (D) NC	222
Clement, Bob (D) TN	2229
Clinger, William (R) PA	2160
Clyburn, James (D) SC	319
Coble, Howard (R) NC	403
Coburn, Tom (R) OK	511
Coleman, Ronald (D) TX	2312
Collins, Barbara-Rose (D) MI	401
Collins, Cardiss (D) IL	2308
Collins, Mac (R) GA	1130
Combest, Larry (R) TX	1511
Condit, Gary (D) CA	2444

Name	Room
Conyers, John (D) MI	2426
Cooley, Wes (R) OR	1609
Costello, Jerry (D) IL	2454
Cox, Christopher (R) CA	2402
Coyne, William (D) PA	2455
Cramer, Bud (D) AL	236
Crane, Phillip (R) IL	233
Crapo, Michael (R) ID	437
Cremeans, Frank (R) OH	1630
Cubin, Barbara (R) WY	1114
Cunningham, Duke (R) CA	227
Danner. Patsy Ann(D) MO	1323
Davis, Thomas (R) VA	415
Deal, Nathan (R) GA	1406
DeFazio, Peter (D) OR	2134
de la Garza, Kika (D) TX	1401
DeLauro, Rosa (D) CT	436
DeLay, Tom (R) TX	203
Dellums, Ronald (D) CA	2108
Deutsch, Peter (D) FL	204
Diaz-Balart, Lincoln (R) FL	431
Dickey, Jay (R) AR	230
Dicks, Norm (D) WA	2467
Dingell, John (D) MI	2328
Dixon, Julian (D) CA	2252
Doggett, Lloyd (D) TX	126
Dooley, Calvin (D) CA	1227
Doolittle, John (R) CA	1526
Dornan, Robert (R) CA	1201
Doyle, Michael (D) PA	1218
Dreier, David (R) CA	411
Duncan, John (R) TN	2400
Dunn, Jennifer (R) WA	432
Durbin, Richard (D) IL	2463
Edwards, Chet (D) TX	328
Ehlers, Vernon (R) MI	1717
Ehrlich, Robert (R) MD	315
Emerson, Bill (R) MO	2268
Engel, Eliot (D) NY	1433
English, Philip (R) PA	1721
Ensign, John (R) NV	414
Eshoo, Anna (D) CA	308
Evans, Lane (D) IL	2335
Everett, Terry (R) AL	208
Ewing, Thomas (R) IL	1317
Farr, Sam (D) CA	1117
Fattah, Chaka (D) PA	1205
Fawell, Harris (R) IL	2159
Fazio, Vic (D) CA	2113
Fields, Cleo (D) LA	218
Fields, Jack (R) TX	2228
Filner, Bob (D) CA	504
Flake Floyd (D) NY	1035
Flanagan Michael (R) IL	1407
Foglietta, Thomas (D) PA	341

Name	Room
Foley, Mark (R) FL	506
Forbes, Michael (R) NY	502
Ford, Harold (D) TN	2111
Fowler, Tillie Kidd (R) FL	413
Fox, Jon (R) PA	510
Frank, Barney (D) MA	2210
Franks, Gary (R) CT	133
Franks, Robert (R) NJ	429
Frazer, Victor (I) VI	1711
Frelinghuysen, R (R) NJ	514
Frisa, Daniel (R) NY	1529
Frost, Martin (D) TX	2459
Funderburk, David (R) NC	427
Furse, Elizabeth (D) OR	316
Gallegly, Elton (R) CA	2441
Ganske, Greg (R) IA	1108
Gejdenson, Sam (D) CT	2416
Gekas, George (R) PA	2410
Gephardt, Richard (D) MO	1226
Geren, Pete (D) TX	2448
Gibbons, Sam (D) FL	2204
Gilchrest, Wayne (R) MD	332
Gillmor, Paul (R) OH	1203
Gilman, Benjamin (R) NY	2449
Gingrich, Newt (R) GA	2428
Gonzalez, Henry (D) TX	2413
Goodlatte, Robert (R) VA	123
Goodling, William (R) PA	2263
Gordon, Bart (D) TN	2201
Goss, Porter (R) FL	108
Graham, Lindsey (R) SC	1429
Green, Gene (D) TX	1024
Greenwood, James (R) PA	430
Gundeson, Steven (R) WI	2185
Gutierrez, Luis (D) IL	408
Gutknecht, Gil (R) MN	425
Hall, Ralph (D) TX	2236
Hall, Tony (D) OH	1432
Hamilton, Lee (D) IN	2314
Hancock, Melton (R) MO	438
Hansen, James (R) UT	2466
Harman, Jane (D) CA	325
Hastert, Dennis (R) IL	2453
Hastings, Alcee Lamar (D) FL	1039
Hastings, Richard 'Doc' (R) WA	1229
Hayes, James (D) LA	2432
Hayworth, J.D. (R) AZ	1023
Hefley, Joel (R) CO	2351
Hefner, Bill (D) NC	2470
Heineman, F.K. (R) NC	1440
Herger, Wally (R) CA	2433
Hilleary, Van (R) TN	114
Hilliard, Earl (D) AL	1002
Hinchey, Maurice (D) NY	1524
Hobson, David (R) OH	1514

Name	Room
Hoekstra, Peter (R) MI	1122
Hoke, Martin (R) OH	212
Holden, Tim (D) PA	1421
Horn, Steve (R) CA	129
Hostettler, John (R) IN	1404
Houghton, Amory (R) NY	1110
Hoyer, Steny (D) MD	1705
Hunter, Duncan (R) CA	2265
Hutchinson, Tim (R) AR	1005
Hyde, Henry (R) IL	2110
Inglis, Bob (R) SC	1237
Istook, Ernest Jim (R) OK	119
Jackson Lee, Sheila (D) TX	1520
Jacobs, Andrew (D) IN	2313
Jefferson, William J (D) LA	240
Johnson, Eddie Bernice (D) TX	1123
Johnson, Nancy (R) CT	343
Johnson, Sam (R) TX	1030
Johnson, Tim (D) SD	2438
Johnston, Harry (D) FL	2458
Jones, Walter B (R) NC	214
Kanjorski, Paul (D) PA	2429
Kaptur, Marcy (D) OH	2104
Kasich, John (R) OH	1131
Kelly, Susan (R) NY	1037
Kennedy, Joseph P (D) MA	2242
Kennedy, Patrick (D) RI	1505
Kennelly, Barbara (D) CT	201
Kildee, Dale (D) MI	2187
Kim, Jay (R) CA	435
King, Peter (R) NY	224
Kingston, Jack (R) GA	1507
Kleczka, Gerald (D) WI	2301
Klink, Ron (D) PA	125
Klug, Scott (R) WI	1113
Knollenberg, Joseph (R) MI	1221
Kolbe, Jim (R) AZ	205
LaFalce, John (D) NY	2310
LaHood, Ray (R) IL	329
Lantos, Tom (D) CA	2217
Largent, Steve (R) OK	410
Latham, Tom (R) IA	516
LaTourette, Steven (R) OH	1508
Laughlin, Greg (R) TX	442
Lazio, Rick (R) NY	314
Leach, James (R) IA	2186
Levin, Sander (D) MI	2230
Lewis, Jerry (R) CA	2112
Lewis, John (D) GA	229
Lewis, Ron (R) KY	412
Lightfoot, Jim Ross (R) IA	2161
Lincoln, Blanche L (D) AR	1204
Linder, John (R) GA	1318
Lipinski, William (D) IL	1501
Livingston, Robert (R) LA	2406

Name	Room
LoBiondo, Frank (R) NJ	513
Lofgren, Zoe (D) CA	118
Longley, James (R) ME	226
Lowey, Nita (D) NY	2421
Lucas, Frank (R) OK	107
Luther, William (D) MN	1419
Maloney, Carolyn (D) NY	1504
Manton, Thomas (D) NY	2235
Manzullo, Donald (R) IL	426
Markey, Edward (D) MA	2133
Martinez, Matthew (D) CA	2239
Martini, Bill (R) NJ	1513
Mascara, Frank (D) PA	1531
Matsui, Robert (D) CA	2311
McCarthy, Karen (D) MO	1232
McCollum, Bill (R) FL	2266
McCrery, Jim (R) LA	225
McDade, Joseph (R) PA	2107
McDermott, James (D) WA	2349
McHale, Paul (D) PA	217
McHugh, John (R) NY	416
McInnis, Scott (R) CO	215
McIntosh, David (R) IN	1208
McKeon, Howard 'Buck' (R) CA	307
McKinney, Cynthia Ann (D) GA	124
McNulty, Michael (D) NY	2442
Meehan, Martin (D) MA	318
Meek, Carrie (D) FL	404
Menendez, Robert (D) NJ	1730
Metcalf, Jack (R) WA	507
Meyers, Jan (R) KS	2303
Mfume, Kweisi (D) MD	2419
Mica, John (R) FL	336
Miller, F Daniel (R) FL	117
Miller, George E. (D) CA	2205
Minge, David (D) MN	1415
Mink, Patsy (D) HI	2135
Moakley, John Joseph (D) MA	235
Molinari, Susan (R) NY	2435
Mollohan, Alan (D) WV	2427
Montgomery, 'Sonny' (D) MS	2184
Moorhead, Carlos (R) CA	2346
Moran, James (D) VA	405
Morella, Constance (R) MD	106
Murtha, John (D) PA	2423
Myers, John (R) IN	2372
Myrick, Sue (R) NC	509
Nadler, Jerrold (D) NY	109
Neal, Richard (D) MA	2431
Nethercutt, George (R) WA	1527
Neumann, Mark (R) WI	1725
Ney, Bob (R) OH	1605
Norwood, Charlie (R) GA	1707
Nussle, Jim (R) IA	303
Oberstar, James (D) MN	2366

Name	Room
Obey, David (D) WI	2462
Oliver, John (D) MA	1027
Ortiz, Solomon (D) TX	2136
Orton, Bill (D) UT	440
Owens, Major (D) NY	2305
Oxley, Michael (R) OH	2233
Packard, Ronald (R) CA	2162
Pallone, Frank (D) NJ	420
Parker, Mike (D) MS	2445
Pastor, Ed (D) AZ	223
Paxon, William (R) NY	2436
Payne, Donald (D) NJ	2244
Payne, Lewis (D) VA	2412
Pelosi, Nancy (D) CA	2457
Peterson, Colin (D) MN	1314
Peterson, Douglas 'Pete' (D) FL	306
Petri, Thomas (R) WI	2262
Pickett, Owen (D) VA	2430
Pombo, Richard (R) CA	1519
Pomeroy, Earl (D) ND	1533
Porter, John Edward (R) IL	2373
Portman, Rob (R) OH	238
Poshard, Glenn (D) IL	2334
Pryce, Deborah (R) OH	221
Quillen, Jimmy (R) TN	102
Quinn, Jack (R) NY	331
Radanovich, George (R) CA	313
Rahall, Nick Joe (D) WV	2269
Ramstad, Jim (R) MN	103
Rangel, Charles (D) NY	2354
Reed, John F 'Jack' (D) RI	1510
Regula, Ralph (R) OH	2309
Richardson, Bill (D) NM	2209
Riggs, Frank (R) CA	1714
Rivers, Lynn Nancy (D) MI	1116
Roberts, Pat (R) KS	1126
Roemer, Timothy (D) IN	407
Rogers, Harold (R) KY	2468
Rohrabacher, Dana (R) CA	2338
Ros-Lehtinen, Ileana (R) FL	2440
Rose, Charles (D) NC	242
Roth, Toby (R) WI	2234
Roukema, Marge (R) NJ	2469
Roybal-Allard, Lucille (D) CA	324
Royce, Edward (R) CA	1133
Rush, Bobby (D) IL	131
Sabo, Martin Olav (D) MN	2336
Salmon, Matt (R) AZ	115
Sanders, Bernard (I) VT	213
Sanford, Mark (R) SC	1223
Sawyer, Thomas (D) OH	1414
Saxton, H. James (R) NJ	339
Scarborough, Joe (R) FL	1523
Schaefer, Dan (R) CO	2353
Schiff, Steven (R) NM	2404

Name	Room
Schroeder, Patricia (D) CO	2307
Schumer, Charles (D) NY	2211
Scott, Robert (D) VA	501
Seastrand, Andrea (R) CA	320
Sensenbrenner, F James (R) WI	2332
Serrano, Jose (D) NY	2342
Shadegg, John (R) AZ	503
Shaw, E Clay (R) FL	2267
Shays, Christopher (R) CT	1502
Shuster, Bud (R) PA	2188
Sisisky, Norman (D) VA	2371
Skaggs, David (D) CO	1124
Skeen, Joe R (R) NM	2367
Skelton, Ike (D) MO	2227
Slaughter, Louise M (D) NY	2347
Smith, Christopher (R) NJ	2370
Smith, Lamar (R) TX	2443
Smith, Linda (R) WA	1217
Smith, Nick (R) MI	1530
Solomon, Gerald (R) NY	2206
Souder, Mark E (R) IN	508
Spence, Floyd (R) SC	2405
Spratt, John (D) SC	1536
Stark, Fortney 'Pete' (D) CA	239
Stearns, Clifford (R) FL	2352
Stenholm, Charles (D) TX	1211
Stockman, Steve (R) TX	417
Stokes, Louis (D) OH	2365
Studds, Gerry (D) MA	237
Stump, Bob (R) AZ	211
Stupak, Bart (D) MI	317
Talent, James (R) MO	1022
Tanner, John (D) TN	1127
Tate, Randy (R) WA	1118
Tauzin, Billy (R) LA	2183
Taylor, Charles (R) NC	231
Taylor, Gene (D) MS	2447
Tejeda, Frank (D) TX	323
Thomas, William (R) CA	2208
Thompson, Bennie (D) MS	1408
Thornberry, Wm. 'Mac' (R) TX	1535
Thornton, Ray (D) AR	1214
Thurman, Karen (D) FL	130
Tiahrt, Todd (R) KS	1319
Torkildsen, Peter (R) MA	120
Torres, Esteban E. (D) CA	2368
Torricelli, Robert (D) NJ	1026
Towns, Edolphus (D) NY	2232
Traficant, James (D) OH	2446
Tucker, Walter (D) CA	419
Upton, Fred (R) MI	2333
Velazquez, Nydia (D) NY	132
Vento, Bruce (D) MN	2304
Visclosky, Peter (D) IN	2464
Volkmer, Harold (D) MO	2409

Name	Room
Vucanovich, Barbara (R) NV	2202
Waldholtz, Enid (R) UT	515
Walker, Robert (R) PA	2369
Walsh, James (R) NY	1330
Wamp, Zach (R) TN	423
Ward, Mike (D) KY	1032
Waters, Maxine (D) CA	330
Watt, Melvin (D) NC	1230
Watts, Julius C 'J.C.' (R) OK	1713
Waxman, Henry (D) CA	2408
Weldon, Curt (R) PA	2452
Weldon, Dave (R) FL	216
Weller, Gerald 'Jerry' (R) IL	1710
White, Rick (R) WA	116

Name	Room
Whitfield, Edward (R) KY	1541
Wicker, Roger (R) MS	206
Williams, Pat (D) MT	2329
Wilson,Charles (D) TX	2256
Wise, Robert (D) WV	2434
Wolf, Frank (R) VA	241
Woolsey, Lynn (D) CA	439
Wyden, Ron (D) OR	1111
Wynn, Albert R (D) MD	418
Yates, Sidney (D) IL	2109
Young, C W Bill (R) FL	2407
Young, Don (R) AK	2331
Zeliff, William (R) NH	1210
Zimmer, Richard (R) NJ	228

104th Congress
United States Senate

Mail is addressed to the building --

- Room number beginning with S only, Capitol Building
- Room number beginning with SD, Dirksen Building
- Room number beginning with SH, Hart Building
- Room number beginning with SR, Russell Building

Mail to your Representative, Bldg Name, Rm No., Washington, DC 20510.

Senators

Name	Room
Abraham, Spencer (R) MI	SD B40-4
Akaka, Daniel (D) HI	SH-720
Ashcroft, John (R) MO	SH-705
Baucus, Max (D) MT	SH-511
Bennett, Robert (R) UT	SD-241
Biden, Joseph (D) DE	SR-221
Bingaman, Jeff (D) NM	SH-110
Bond, Christopher (R) MO	SR-293
Boxer, Barbara (D) CA	SH-112
Bradley, Bill (D) NJ	SH-731
Breaux, John (D) LA	SH-516
Brown, Hank (R) CO	SH-716
Bryan, Richard (D) NV	SR-364
Bumpers, Dale (D) AR	SD-229
Burns, Conrad (R) MT	SD-183
Byrd, Robert (D) WV	SH-311
Campbell, Ben N (R) CO	SR-380
Chafee, John (R) RI	SD-567
Coats, Dan (R) IN	SR-404
Cochran, Thad (R) MS	SR-326
Cohen, William (R) ME	SH-322
Conrad, Kent (D) ND	SH-724
Coverdell, Paul (R) GA	SR-200

Name	Room
Craig, Larry (R) ID	SH-313
D'Amato, Alfonse (R) NY	SH-520
Daschle, Thomas (D) SD	SH-317
DeWine, Mike (R) OH	SR-140
Dodd, Christopher (D) CT	SR-444
Dole, Robert (R) KS	SH-141
Domenici, Pete (R) NM	SD-328
Dorgan, Byron (D) ND	SH-713
Exon, James (D) NE	SH-528
Faircloth, M. 'Lauch' (R) NC	SH-702
Feingold, Russell (D) WI	SH-502
Feinstein, Dianne (D) CA	SH-331
Ford, Wendell (D) KY	SR-173A
Frist, William (R) TN	SH-825
Glenn, John (D) OH	SH-503
Gore, Al (D) TN PRESIDENT	SD-202
Gorton, Slade (R) WA	SH-730
Graham, Bob (D) FL	SH-524
Gramm, Phil (R) TX	SR-370
Grams, Rod (R) MN	SD B40-3
Grassley, Charles (R) IA	SH-135
Gregg, Judd (R) NH	SR-393
Harkin, Tom (D) IA	SH-531

Name	Room
Hatch, Oren (R) UT	SR-135
Hatfield, Mark (R) OR	SH-711
Heflin, Howell (D) AL	SH-728
Helms, Jesse (R) NC	SD-403
Hollings, Ernest (D) SC	SR-125
Hutchison, Kay (R) TX	SH-703
Inhofe, James (R) OK	SR-453
Inouye, Daniel (D) HI	SH-722
Jeffords, James (R) VT	SH-513
Johnston, J Bennett (D) LA	SH-136
Kassebaum, Nancy L (R) KS	SR-302
Kempthorne, Dirk (R) ID	SD-367
Kennedy, Edward (D) MA	SR-315
Kerry, J Robert (D) NE	SH-303
Kerry, John (D) MA	SR-421
Kohl, Herbert (D) WI	SH-330
Kyl, Jon (R) AZ	SR-363
Lautenberg, Frank (D) NJ	SH-506
Leahy, Patrick (D) VT	SR-433
Levin, Carl (D) MI	SR-459
Lieberman, Joseph (D) CT	SH-316
Lott, Trent (R) MS	SR-487
Lugar, Richard (R) IN	SH-306
Mack, Connie (R) FL	SH-517
McCain, John (R) AZ	SR-111
McConnell, Mitch (R) KY	SR-120
Mikulski, Barbara (D) MD	SH-709
Moseley-Braun, Carol (D) IL	SH-320
Moynihan, Daniel P (D) NY	SR-464
Murkowski, Frank (R) AK	SH-706
Murray, Patty (D) WA	SH-302
Nickles, Don (R) OK	SH-133
Nunn, Sam (D) GA	SD-303
Pell, Claiborne (D) RI	SR-335
Pressler, Larry (R) SD	SR-243
Pryor, David (D) AR	SR-267
Reid, Harry (D) NV	SH-324
Robb, Charles (D) VA	SR-493
Rockefeller, John D (D) WV	SH-109
Roth, William (R) DE	SH-104
Santorum, Rick (R) PA	SD B40-2
Sarbanes, Paul (D) MD	SH-309
Shelby, Richard (R) AL	SH-509
Simon, Paul (D) IL	SD-462
Simpson, Alan (R) WY	SD-105
Smith, Robert (R) NH	SD-332
Snowe, Olympia (R) ME	SR-174
Specter, Arlen (R) PA	SH-530
Stevens, Ted (R) AK	SH-522
Thomas, Craig (R) WY	SD-B34
Thompson, Fred (R) TN	SD-523
Thurmond, Strom (R) SC	SR-217
Warner, John (R) VA	SR-225
Wellstone, Paul (D) MN	SH-717

DEPARMENT OF THE INTERIOR
1849 C Street, N.W.
Washington, DC 20240
Secretary of the Interior: Bruce Babbitt
Ass't Secretary: George T. Frampton, Jr.

DEPARTMENT OF AGRICULTURE
Administration Building
14th St. and Independence Ave S.W.
Washington, DC 20250
Deputy Secretary: Richard E. Rominger
Forest Service Chief: Jack Ward Thomas
Natural Resources Chief: Paul W. Johnson

US HOUSE STANDING COMMITTEES
Washington, DC 20515

AGRICULTURE
1301 Longworth Building
Chairman: Pat Roberts (R) KS

APPROPRIATIONS
H218 Capitol Building
Chairman: Robert Livingston (R) LA

RESOURCES
1324 Longworth Building
Chairman: Don Young (R) AK

COMMERCE
2125 Rayburn Building
Chairman: Thomas Bliley (R) VA

US SENATE STANDING COMMITTEES
Washington, DC 20510

AGRICULTURE, NUTRITION AND FORESTRY
328A Russell Building
Chairman: Richard Lugar (R) IN

APPROPRIATIONS
S 128 Capitol Building
Chairman: Mark Hatfield (R) OR

BUDGET
621 Dirksen Building
Chairman: Pete Domenici (R) NM

ENERGY AND NATURAL RESOURCES
364 Dirksen Building
Chairman: Frank Murkowski (R) AK

ENVIRONMENT AND PUBLIC WORKS
458 Dirksen Building
Chairman: John Chafee (R) RI

A GREAT GIFT IDEA

Let your friends, co-workers, employees and neighbors learn about the "horrors" of the Endangered Species Act. Enlighten them to the costs -- economic, constitutional and environmental -- and the uncompensated "takings" of private property. Let them see how the Act "works", and of the solutions to "a law gone haywire". Send for additional copies today. ONLY $12.95 each plus S & H.

Now only $12.95 plus $3.00 S & H each
Allow 4-6 weeks delivery

FREE SHIPPING on Orders of 5 or more

- -

Name_____Phone_____

Street_____City_____

State_____Zip_____

\# Copies_____X $12.95 = $_____.____   Mail Check to:

\# Copies_____X $ 3.00 = $_____   Whitney-Hill
           shipping   P.O. Box 2910
   7.25% CA sales tax = $_____   Santa Rosa, CA
                  95405

      Total = $_____